PATTI Z.
THIS IS ME

At my Lake Point home, this was the archway and pathway leading to the gardens, fountain and mystical village in the distance, near Cedar Lake and Dean Parkway. We are to appreciate and take care of...

PATTI Z.
THIS IS ME

*An art book to awaken and
enhance the creative life naturally*

WWW.PATTIZONA.COM

Copyright © 2020 Patti Zona

978-1-952874-38-3 (paperback)
978-1-952874-39-0 (hardback)
978-1-952874-40-6 (eBook)

All rights reserved. No part of this publication may be reproduced, stored in a retrieval system, or transmitted in any form or by any means - electronic, mechanical, photocopy, recording, scanning, or other – except for brief quotations in critical reviews or articles, without the prior written permission of the publisher.

Printed in New York by:

OMNIBOOK CO.
99 Wall Street, Suite 118
New York, NY 10005
USA
+1-866-216-9965
www.omnibookcompany.com

For e-book purchase: Kindle on Amazon, Barnes and Noble
Book purchase: Amazon.com, Barnes & Noble, and
www.omnibookcompany.com

Omnibook titles may be purchased in bulk for educational, business, fund-raising, or sales promotional use. For more information please e-mail **info@omnibookcompany.com**

Designed by: Gian Carlo Tan

Dedication

As I have said before or written before--this is dedicated to the ones' I love. And, that is for sure. I want to dedicate this book also to those who love the arts, beautiful works of art and those who try in ernest. And, the music that heals, to music you feel, that thrills and makes you want to move to the rhythm. I would like to dedicate this book to my friends Cammy, Jill, Betsy and my godchild Genevieve. Karen and Bob in Southbend, Indiana, Janice and Tim Woods, Karen and Fred Walker, Armen, Ara, Nathan Barbara and Francis, Red and Lorraine all the way to Vermont. Stacey, Sean and Maggie lost and found. Bob "Gilby" Gilbertson, Georgia and Bob are all so special. And of course, Paul and Mary, and Richard for too long, it's time, and all my children. You know who you are plus Michael and Therese, Joseph, Lucia, Zoe and Vince, Melissa and Jenna and now Tony and Liam. Love you all. I moved to this wonderful place. It's like a community surrounded with angels of all shapes and sizes, personalities plus, wise beyond , kind and caring with a sense of humor too. I'll name a few Judy C, Helene, Marion, Linda, Ruth, Marybeth, Jerri, Corrine, Faye, Ginger, Jan, Sandy, Bill and Betty, Tom and Heather, Audrey, Barb, Charlie and Jack, Kristin, Polly, Amy and Deanne. Here's to you Barb N. and Cherl and Rose too. Danny Seipp, Andy and Gian are stars! You all did a good job! And also to Linda from Little Shop (where I got my jacket and top--another friend), and of course to Linhoff Photography Studio.

But, I also want to dedicate this book to those who are no longer here or with us. As I think of my mother and father in law Diva and Alfred were like my own. They were so special and so dearly loved. I miss them. Aunt Elda and Uncle John. Aunt Lorraine and Uncle George. I hope you like being in a book. But, then I think of my own parents, who are no longer here also. I feel a sorrow of a different kind. My sister Sandy. I wish you were here. My dear friend and tennis partner Barb Hagan, Jackie and Mark Hegman, Rita Nelson way too soon. This is dedicated to you and more. I am humbled and tired, I dedicate this to our Father in Heaven, Prince of Peace, Jesus our Savior and our Creator be with us always. Guide us throughout this life.

Audrey, Rita, Me (I cut my own hair) and Ruth

Ruth, Linda, Me, Rita and Audrey

Judy and Me

Nancy, Barb, Linda, Halene, and Molly

Jerri, Mike, Ruth, Charlie, Molly, Marian, Sally, Me and Halene

Jan, Me, Halene, Barb, Jean and Molly

Acknowledgments

Writing about my creative life in these times, many times seemed surreal. I felt removed from what was happening around me. And, I was--removed. Everyone was affected in ways that grew into something new. Everyday. Every week. Grew into months. But, it was never just about the pandemic, but the erosion of our conscience, our values and principles, the excess and then the need for more, or greater, or faster than before. Forever changing, so constantly adapting and then accepting. Even if only momentarily.

At first this pandemic allowed me a space of time, but then what was happening around me and everyone was so unbelievable that I felt fortunate to have a project to focus on. When things turned from bad to worse, I felt a responsibility once move--wake up the apathetic. Demand change. Insist on the hierarchy to be the leaders that are needed instead of reaping the benefits, high on their pedestal. Untouched, Unscathed. Seemingly unfazed. The divide has grown deeper, wider too. United we stand. Divided we fall. Once taken seriously. Now forgotten in it's meaning. For people no longer want to think that much or too deep or for too long.

These experiences instead of learning from them seemed to bring out the worst, in the most unexpected way and from the most unexpected people. And so many. It does seem an impossible task, or an impossible endeavor at times. But, I still won't believe that. The result at the end is worth working toward. But, it is going to take time, Precious time. But we can make it productive and worthwhile. So for this reason, we have to rise above it all. Overcome and show we can make a better difference and learn from this fiasco. We all have to learn to work together and appreciate instead of letting inflated egos rule and ruin. We can't let that happen.

Now, I want to thank all of my friends, new friends and friends from years gone by. Much too quickly. When I have talked of a creative life--I mean living creatively too. Don't get stuck in such a routine that has become unbending that you no longer feel the need to get out of the box or think beyond the moment. Start with breaking a bad habit. Develop a new skill. And, then teach others what you excel in. If they are interested or could enhance their life. Take care of yourself, your family and friends for they are a blessing and a gift. I do want to thank all who have stressed such fervent interest in my endeavors that inspires me further. I want that for you too. But, when I am tired, doubting and weary I am grateful for my health, my mind and faith that our Father in Heaven will watch over us all. Protect and Guide.

A book of inspiration to find your creative self
Writing in these times. Painting in a former time.

So, it is amazing the wonderful things we all can do? We can do works of art of many varieties, even extraordinary majestic sculptures, or at least an interesting piece—that we prize and treasure. Not everyone has their own piece of sculpture in their home or their parent's home. For a gift from the heart you have created, made yourself is a special treasure for the home or the gardens. It is lasting too. When anyone looks at it, they will always think of you, remarkable you. One of these days, I will make my own piece of sculpture. Or throw a pot of clay, throughout the day. Have a collection. But this book is about my paintings. I usually worked in oils. Oils have many dimensions smooth and light as many watercolors can achieve. Or if you need or prefer oil can create a variety of textures. Acrylics and oils are similar except acrylics are water based. Oils are known for its durability and melding quality and lasting ability.

It is interesting to discover texture. Even more impelling is to learn how to achieve the effects by using different brushes to pallet knives. It is a great way to bring a canvas to life, almost real. Wanting to touch, feel the texture. One of my first works of art was a forest scene, creating the bark of the tree with a sliver of the palette knife. Worked so well that I did the boulders also, with shades of taupe with a touch of white and various highlights for added interest. Oh, I dappled the leaves on the tree, with different shades of greens. The leaves gently touched the mottled shade to the sun. It works better if you work from the top down. Start with a light wash and gradually build. You paint what you see. The more you paint, the more you see. The end result is what will be. And, if an extra touch is needed, you can ever so gently add some dry brushing. It is training your eye, your touch that adds so much and makes you complete your own treasured piece.

For some reason we never thought or maybe we were never taught the importance of incorporating creativity in our daily life. Maybe we were even told that we were not that creative or even that talented, certainly not an artist. But you would be pleasantly surprised, just being introduced and envisioning the possibilities. For we all continue to learn when we are ready or inspired. When there is a hint of inspiration that simmers and grows. If you have a certain amount of time, why not give it a try, given the chance, the right instructions, the proper provisions such as palette knives of various sizes, assorted brushes of good quality. Sometimes even the right equipment or outfit. Having an easel set up, with natural lighting—will inspire. So, ready to go. Well at least be comfortable and free to be—your creative self. Think about it. Give it some thought. Where and how to begin. Envision being in that creative atmosphere.

Anything is possible. Especially when we aspire for the good and appreciate the wonders and beauty that surrounds us. We want to be part of the grandeur. Make it inviting and lasting. Therefore, it is important before you begin your actual painting to prepare your canvas with a wash of a small amount of a light mix of Oil Paint and linseed oil, different types of oils will give a certain finish. Take time to explore the local art stores and inquire what is needed so you will be prepared. From the type of medium. Will it be Oils, Acrylics, Pastels to Watercolor? For oil paints, you will need turpentine to clean your brushes and sometimes yourself. Now there are non-toxic turpentines and oils. But I still do not taste it. Sometimes, we become so engrossed, absorbed even captivated in the subject matter that we forget we have our paintbrush in hand.

Your subject matter. The subject you are to paint does matter. For me it was the challenge of recreating a painting that I was drawn to. Out of curiosity. Could I do it? That was also part of my learning tool. But later, I wanted to create my own works of art. I wanted to bring beauty into my home, as well as introducing some culture to my children / family. To be an inspiration to them. "If my mom can paint and do and accomplish. Then I can and will too." It was my young way of thinking. Not jaded or faded. Never forgotten. And it is true, there must be a spark of real reason and purpose for we are given these gifts to be used for the good. I wanted to bring beauty into my home and the lives of my children that would not require a vast amount of money or time. Except, some paintings did require more time than others. The interesting things for me—I became more organized. For, I still had a busy household. Children needing attention and attending, meals put on the table, later prepare for the lunch box. They usually liked my lunches. When off at school or nap time. I would straighten up, tidy up, throw a load of laundry in the washer. And gravitate to my easel where I would step back and wonder and ponder. How to achieve the desired effect. At least, I had ideas of how to achieve and do and still be productive. The kids loved it.

I had my easel set up in a corner by a window. That was a must. During the day, I would always be busy amidst the distractions of various kinds. For I felt my responsibilities of my family and my house- hold chores came first. Yet lingering in the back of mind would be thoughts of getting back to my painting seeing the kid's reaction to progress made. When coming home or waking up, depending on the subject matter the first thing the kids were drawn to see was my painting placed on my easel. The progress made, seeing the changes, I hoped always to inspire. In those early years, between schedules and duties always prevalent—my painting became a welcoming treat. Not just for myself but my children also. That is when I was most prolific in my painting. For it seemed, I was always surrounded by incentive, desire and ability that kept growing. That is one of the beauties of a creative spirit. Inspires beyond even when not aware.

My husband traveled early on, in our marriage. It was just accepted. Between his travels and our children, I knew it was important that both our lives were fulfilling. It was important for our children also. In the absence of their father, I would have to be content within myself. After all, we had two young sons and eventually a baby daughter at this time in life. Yet, I still felt fortunate. Rick did provide what was important to him. I would provide what he could not. Which would be a loving and inviting home for our children and of course for him and myself. We were a family doing what was expected and needed. It was and still is the most important role one can do. For that time in life is so fleeting. At any rate…

Because of those travels, many times, after the day was done and the children in bed, I would do most of my painting when the children were asleep. Rick was doing what he was educated to do with growing successes. In my marriage, I was. I always felt safe and secure in those times. How lucky could I be to have three children inquisitive, sometimes precocious which is natural and normal, occasionally challenging. So never a dull moment. But mostly happy and healthy. All unique and precious. With all those wonderful traits, I had incredible incentives to do and be.

And now I am given the opportunity and encouragement to further some of my own goals. Within limits. For then, I was married with responsibilities that would shape our future. I loved my husband. Our little family. Our reason and purpose, depending on both of us to provide. I was fortunate because I also had talents and abilities that I could use and improve from our home base. We both had our incentives. Our children. I wanted to provide the best atmosphere in our home to thrive. Isn't that what we all want? If only we could turn back the clock. Turn back time. For time is so fleeting.

It seemed life was more predictable back then. We had a routine that worked. And was accepted. Just made life easier than the unexpected or lack of a routine which of course would occur periodically. But that is to be expected within a family and life. So, be prepared. Have the necessities taken care of as the day wanes or winds down. Bathes, pajamas, teeth brushed-- at bedtime, I would always tuck them in with a story or maybe a sweet lullaby. For some reason, the kids liked that. When they were nestled in their beds. I would put some music on and work on my painting. Depending on the subject matter—some works were more energizing and some placid and soothing. I would put the music on soft so as not to disturb. I would paint to beautiful classical, even rock, sometimes jazz—depending on the mood or ambiance or the subject matter.

To me doing a beautiful portrait needed a beautiful classical piece—say Moonlight Sonata. Seascapes with crashing waves would need a great orchestral piece. Something that provided the impetus and energy for dramatic, sweeping strokes to heighten the spirit and vigor from decrescendo to crescendo into magnificence. Many times, a piece of music provides what we cannot provide. Or dare to tread.

I loved doing seascapes, clipper ships high on the waves. Sail boats too. Florals were a test for me. I loved the colors, the arrangements sometimes formal and gracious other times homey and comforting. To be displayed. I also enjoyed painting portraiture. I have done several. Occasionally I would do big cats, leopards with spots, stripes and of course the regal lion. Landscapes are a must to paint. I have never done a snow scene but one day I shall. I have painted a variety of subjects for each of which has its own lesson to teach. And I am still learning.

We cannot all be artists. And most of us will never be a famous singer, dancer, artiste or missionary. But those gifts and talents are in the soul of all of us. Those gifts of abilities help sustain throughout the day. Throughout life. Giving us a little reprieve from all the responsibilities that have become too much, too many and growing nonstop. And are we happier for it? When did it become our responsibility to pick up the pieces of the chaos left behind from the irresponsible and reckless or the entitled? For that, I am curious. When and how did good intentions turn? No longer honorable or worthy. When do we realize, enough is enough? Too much of anything, gets lost in the shuffle of life. Striving for so long and the goal is reached. It feels good to attain. This would have been the time to let go of the reins, turn it over to fresh hands. Try something new for a healthier balance. For to sustain is a different entity. The goal has been reached to the peak. It is not quite what we thought. We want to strive further, for more. Sounds like an addiction. And it is-- of a different kind. It is too bad we put so much trust in others that we no longer even know our own strength but get lost in the crowd. We never want to perpetuate the madness.

I know this book is to be an art book. A book that inspires the creative spirit. And that is what I want to convey and eventually achieve. But for much too long. It seems life has become more about survival, trying to make ends meet and trying to understand the underlying cause of the uncertainty, inequity, the troubling discontent along with the growing disconnect. Is there any connection here? When did it all begin to unravel, becoming a tangled mess? The beginning is lost and the meaning no longer recognizable. I remember when prayer was no longer permissible in schools or public places. The arts were no longer part of the curriculum. There would no longer be time for recess. And, when small cubicles became the workplace. Breaks were limited. Always on a time clock. The emphasis was always on the bottom line, quantity over quality. The demand to fill that quota for the sake of profit for the company.

Needless to say, "cutting corners when the demands so great were overlooked all the mistakes made and overlooked in their haste--could not help but affect the quality." Because the quantity became the most important objective for the company / corporations. Striving to complete the product or mission left little time for a social life at home or workplace. Our creative life began to suffer in silence. Who in the world has the time? And that is the shame, for our creative gifts are what is needed for all. To do. To be. For others to see and know there is a better way than this hectic pace. Only to achieve other peoples' dreams at the cost of our own.

We cannot give up our gifts or relinquish the best of ourselves for concepts or to those who are not deserving. Yet will take but really do not appreciate it. There are users and abusers and their numbers grow. And the numbers are what they know and want to control. Until the numbers become so many and out of control, then they become unreachable. Absent. Taught to avoid the questions. That is why it is so important to know how to read—to be informed on any and every subject. It is equally important to know how to write—penmanship. Shows a persons' character and another way to represent yourself. To articulate and put pen to paper or a pencil—eraser too. Much more gratifying to see and do.

I need to admit, I do like the computer to write, but I do not like the popups that distract, or having to delete messages before you even begin. Before you know, you need to start the whole process over again. It is possible to use and know how to do both. Be on your toes and in the know, for the new technological gadgets and change are constant having to adapt. And when the power goes out, once again you are stuck. Waiting. If you have pen and paper at hand, the process can begin—again. Taking notes, or writing a letter is always special to receive. Here lately, when I start a note or letter and if I make a small mistake—I will turn that mistake into a flower or scribbled dancer, tennis player or runner or a sailboat on rippling water. Sometimes you find those little scribbles reflect the mood in the moment. It is amazing what you see in your scribbles. Those scribbles or embellishment adds a little more interest, humor and surprise in your notes or letters. Extra special. I do believe.

When life becomes so hectic and serious too, simplify your life. Remember those interests and creative gifts are valuable for a more balanced, healthy and happier life. More fulfilling too. We are not always aware of our abilities or hidden talents even when others know by the way you present yourself, by your speech or your observations, descriptions, a change in persona and new-found enthusiasm. It is rather esoteric, an awakening, simmering, and desire to create, build or express using force not to be held back-- even bursting forth. Waiting to be renewed, attended finally and brought into your life or back into your life to refresh and renew. Those are gifts for a reason to enhance your life. All work and no play, is not a healthy or gratifying way to live. It is easy to get stuck, accepting a routine for that is what we are taught even programmed. We are not a machine or a robot to be programmed—or become one dimensional. It's' not easy to extricate yourself from habits formed in this time of disconnect. For we are scattered. Doing what is needed for survival in the concrete jungle with exclusive new rules that protect the few who will profit. It surprises me but saddens me also for now values have changed. We have become non-stop, excessive. The emphasis now is quantity over quality. The need for more. But not enough time to process life. Are we doing this right? How can we question when the livelihood is at stake? Seems we have stopped growing, learning new skills except what is programmed.

Early morning May 30, 2020…

I wanted to write this book in an atmosphere of contentment and peace. But how could that happen. When I have moved once more. Just in time before everything and everyone was shut down. Almost like a state of limbo. Right now, everyone is in a state of restlessness and uncertainty. Not knowing, not prepared. And afraid. Afraid of getting sick. Afraid of what is to come. Something dire was happening from a distance encroaching closer in your space. Wherever, and whenever. Constant. And insidious. Wanting to be prepared, but impossible when so unknown and unexpected. You could sense it, even fill it in your body and your mind simmering, brewing for much too long. If your senses are drowned in excess, what is happening around will not be felt. At least not as deeply. Out of touch, unaware, without a thought or care. Becoming reckless and careless. Seeing but not knowing from a distance. Making its presence known, in a form of a virus that is unknown without a cure. Social distancing, isolation too, that should work—for weeks, months. It's rampant. Could be a year, eighteen months. Certainly not years. Be aware and prepared. People in a state of fear, even those who are to protect and given a special privilege to enforce their will-- even though the consequences are severe. Unthinkable. Unforgettable and unforgiveable. Now we not only have a pandemic but left with the consequences of actions left unchecked for too long. Anger leads to destruction and reckless actions / behavior. We have not learned or accepted a better way. A more humane way. Why not? Is there a hidden agenda in here somewhere?

I woke early this morning even though I went to bed later than I wanted. But the sun was streaming through the cracks of the opaque shades. I lay there wanting to go back to sleep. But my head was filled with thoughts of the events before. When did this all begin and when will it end? Is it possible that we can learn from these events that were insidiously thrusted upon us? Shouldn't we all be informed? Why can't we learn from those mistakes? Instead we never admit them or address them? We suffer in silence because of our pride. Why don't we speak up to protest immediately when acts of injustices occur repeatedly, over and over again? Until something snaps, breaks

What we are taught but never taught thoroughly and what we do or how we act on presumptions and omissions can cause confusion and tremendous societal problems. Unless that is the purpose. Ignore until the well runs dry. Left in a state of neglect. Forgotten. Turning into rust and dust. But when finally churned the squeaky wheel spoke volumes. And it is not pretty or comforting.

May 31, 2020-- midmorning

What a contrast from yesterday. Prayers were answered. Voices were heard. Compassion was felt. Knowing that a better change was needed for all. These past events opened the door to understanding and making it possible for working together. United in purpose. We can learn from the past, past mistakes finally addressed. But not for long. There was a peaceful protest. Because of all the unrest the night before. Many of us (were told to be safe) just stayed put in our home. Not to go out, except on our own yards, our own balcony, or a short walk. What was much needed for mind, our body and soul. Was a need for reassurance. Hoping the violence had finally stopped, worn itself out. Reassurance is needed for everyone. Violence never helps and never heals. It perpetuates madness. And that is what some have been taught through the years. To lash out, to insight, fuel the fires. Even to hurt and maim. At the time, nothing matters to them. They no longer see the destruction they have left behind. They can no longer feel the pain. Not even their own. For their rage is greater than anything they feel or understand. For now, they are numb. Drained from it all. A little time to refuel their anger into another rage to be released. For those emotions are felt within so deep and for so long. There is no healing balm for them. No answers to their questions from early on. Nothing has changed for them.

Where is the hope when the losses have been one too many and for too long? Living with deprivation, while surrounded with glitz and glamour, excess and opulence but always out of reach. Confusing times. Conflicting laws, rules and regulations which are designed for one reason. And do we know why? Do you believe that it could be to keep the masses down? Is it for even more empowerment, control of the outcome for yourself and others? We have never delved into the root of the problem. We should say problems. Then we would have to take a deep look at ourselves. Our part. Our role. What we have compared to others. What we have shared with others, but not with all.

Why do we stay silent when we should speak up? Why have our basic rights and necessities slowly been eroded without a question or understanding? Just to accept our plight. While those who have much too much spoil and plunder, rape and take and feel so entitled. For their designer rules and laws have been made especially for them. I heard about the license to kill. I have learned about the license to steal if you are wealthy enough.

Corporate America, Wall Street, big and small government and institutions, people in positions of power and wealth—do you understand? Do you not hear or see the damages done by power gone amuck, rampant greed left unchecked and the ugliness of excess? Where is your common sense? Forgotten? Where is your compassion or heart? Is it lost, buried beneath the ruins of the past? Where is the justice in this life when we profit from problems instead of correcting them?

There needs to be a change in structure, when so divided nothing is ever resolved. But for too long, we have lived with such dysfunction and corruption in supposed high places, that we know longer know what is right and what is wrong. Life could be easier and more rewarding if done for the good of all, what is right or the most appropriate for everyone. There needs to be understanding, respect for all life. For we are all one and the same.

In these times we are being tested. Bring out the best in yourself and others will follow. That is our purpose. Simple as that. It is not to have a hierarchy built on destruction of mind, our body and at the cost of our soul. This is the time that we work together. We are all different. But we learn from each other. We all have something unique to give in our growth in life. There is a better way. This is the time to embrace our differences. Use our gifts graciously, with foresight and gratitude. I read recently; a small quote, "I want to love as Jesus loves." Isn't that what we all want? Except to many have forgotten or they never were taught our real meaning in life. But we need to remember and know we can all strive to do and be better than this. Our gifts in this life are to be used for the good. Use your gifts lovingly and wisely. Appreciate and take care to bring out the best in you and others.

Because of these past events, it is difficult to stay on track. That is to write a book on my paintings. To inspire others. For I felt I would have a creative life. That was my saving grace. Yet it would not prevent the intrusions in life caused by the unexpected, for we have all been caught up in the new age of technology. Which should make life easier. We can connect with people from all over the world. Yet, we are stuck to the computer creating a disconnect at home. We should be more reachable, but now drained and removed from what is happening around us. Progress came with a myriad of problems also letting in a darker element like a mask that we are to wear but also offers a disguise. Always a reminder to protect. Not only ourselves, but for the protection of others. It is a simple thing to do.

Yet sometimes we protest too much. As difficult as these times are, I feel it offers a unique opportunity also. To test ourselves. Rise above it all to help make a better difference. Challenge yourself and others to rebuild, restore in creative ways that are healthy. Uniting in purpose. Find your creative spirit in whatever you do.

From the time that I can remember even as a small child. I knew I was to be a singer, dancer, artiste and missionary. I have done all of those and more but not how I expected. Nor even with the support or appreciation that I naturally thought came along with all these abilities or attributes. I would have to find that through myself--in my strong desire, will and determination. For I knew in my heart these gifts would help me all through life. And it did. And it continues.

We all have and need a creative side to get us through those difficult times. It can be as simple as a pot of clay. Sketching or doodling your way to a fun hobby or find a space for a workshop. Find your hidden talent or passion and bring it to life. We need to incorporate some levity, joy, spontaneity in this rhythm of life. Let your garden grow. From sun to shade, perennial to annual. Learn the difference and the need for each. Discover the mysteries and wonders of succulent plants and all the varieties of the cactus. There are plants that climb and flowers on the vine. Ground covers too that spread and grow, but be careful.

They will take over if you lose control. Take a dance class for fun, style and grace or cooking class to nourish and replenish, share and provide. Share your talents that brighten the day and inspire creativity for a better way. Volunteer your time where your heart guides you. Teach others your new skills that have brightened your day. Be the light. Be the inspiration. Everyday do a meaningful act of kindness. This is the time that we know and can show we do have heart. We can learn a better way.

In these following pages, I will present my creative and artistic side that has helped me through those challenging times. Step back. Re-evaluate your life. What is working well and what needs attention or some improvement. What makes us happy or fulfilled with satisfaction and inspiration. And energizes us too in the process of discovery.

This was my first real painting, on canvas a beautiful forest scene. I wanted to duplicate this beautiful forest scene. Could I do it? I was a young mother back then with two young boys. One day, I met one of my neighbors who was an artist. Carla Ballaro. She was gifted, kind and beautiful. We had a conversation one day and I told her I wanted to learn how to paint in oils. She told me, she had a few pupils and I could come and observe. I did just that. Watching and being in that element drew me in. I was so excited knowing the possibilities I had to tell my new friend, Irma Piatoni.

Even though I was a young mother I still aspired to learn and grow with each opportunity. Every morning rain or shine, sleet or snow I would walk my sons' Mark and Duane to the corner to catch their school bus going to St. Rocco school. Irma was surrounded by her young daughters Susie and Donna and sons' Tony and Raymond. All with dark hair except their mom, Irma with wavy short blond hair. Her observing eyes were insightful and kind.

One morning after the kids were safely on the bus we were walking home. Irma tells me, "My daughter Susie looks like she could be your daughter with her dark hair. And your son, Duane looks like he could be my son with his blond hair." That was true. They were cute together, complimenting each other. The same size, compatible and adorable at this young age. My son with blond hair and her little girl, her dark hair braided. So pretty. We became fast friends. She was my first friend at this time in life who had children also. She taught me yoga. And we took tole painting classes together. That is doing decorative painting on wood. I introduced her to Carla Ballaro and our little art class grew by two. We would be two budding artists. Shared friendships with the same goals and love of family. Our impetus.

This forest scene was my first painting. I liked the way the light fell through the trees on the the path. I used thick paint on my brush and a palette knife on the bark of the trees and big rock and grassy areas.

    By this time, I had finished the forest scene. I think back, at how lucky and happy I was back then. My wonderful art class, my new friendship, but also back then, I was taking ballet at the Bonath Twins Studio. Wow, what a wonderful life. But my real reason and purpose were my children—my incentive. I was grounded with purpose and fulfillment. Surrounded with music in my dance and music that moved me to do my paintings. I was there for my children who soaked up the energy to use in work and play throughout the day. I was thinking, where did I find that picture?

    Memories come back, leafing through a magazine. Seeing this forest scene that I would try to reproduce. I cut that picture out of the pages and brought it to my class. I was so fastidious wanting to capture the mottled leaves and texture of the bark of the tree. That you wanted to touch and see if it were real. I wanted to bring the warmth of the sun to the gentle coolness of the shade. The scent of the earth in the forest. That was my first. My first step into knowing and realizing. There is more than we know in that moment in time when we try and go one step further. We just need to be introduced. My son has that painting now.

In that same magazine, I had noticed a picture of an old wooden water mill, painted red. I loved the contrast. The weathered and time-worn water mill now a faded red color against the water trickling down with each turn of the wheel. The contrast of the forest greens captured my attention. Since I had finished a forest scene, that painting would complement that painting and cement my ability in forestry. And another element which was water. When our little family moved to South Bend, I would give my mother and father in law the painting of the red watermill hidden in the forest to my dear mother and father in law. I had already given them a wooden trivet. A tole` painting with the words ``life is just a bowl of cherries" with vines painted bordering the round wooden trivet. My mother in law kept that wooden trivet for it is useful and a reminder of what we shared for many years.

When I saw this seascape I knew I had to try an paint this scene. The turbulent waters in the vast ocean reflecting the colors of the sky. The giant waves crashing to the shores. The soft sands saturated, with pockets of frothy waters. The wet boulders shiny wet. Done with a palette knife.

Shortly after these paintings, there would be talk of moving. Just rumors you know, but still lingered the uncertainty of not knowing when. For me, I knew I needed to paint as many diverse subjects to keep in my memory bank. This was time to use wisely, but also gave me a distraction from feeling the effects of being uprooted. I stumbled upon this beautiful seascape. I brought the picture to my class and there were lots of oohs and ahs.' "Wow, you're going to paint all that?" There is the dramatic sky. Dusk to Sunset. The brilliant colors reflecting on the waters and shore. The crashing waves going on to the shore of the sandy beach to the rocks and boulders. I could feel how I was to reproduce this scene with brushes and paint and now was the time to put my pallet knives to the test. I would use the edge of a straight brush to show the effects of waves rippled to the shore. The pallet knives work beautifully to achieve texture or the gradation on rocks and boulders. There is nothing like inspiration that energizes and compels one forward. Especially when worthwhile.

Now that I knew I had limited time in this special class of instruction I wanted to make it worthwhile. Plus, I liked the challenge but more than that I was inspired by the magnificence. After all, I was born in the town of Neptune by the sea. I diligently prepared my canvas and did a quick wash of what I was to paint. I started that part of the painting in class. When I came home and showed the kids they looked, seemed somewhat impressed and then ran out to play. I would pick up here and there, maybe run the vacuum and start preparing dinner for the kids. My husband was out of town for the week. This time was meant for the kids but also my time. I felt since everything was in order, the boys drifting off to sleep. Now was my time to work on painting the sea.

I quietly set up my easel as not to disturb the kids. There is always a little mixture of nerves and excitement. But once I get into the painting and start seeing the results of the paint on canvas. I feel more confident and competent. This is what I should be doing. I feel at peace with the world and a contentment within. For I have my beautiful family, reason and purpose and the ability to do works of art. As I work my way down from sky to water, my brushes will change for the weight of the water so powerful—I use more paint and eventually my pallet knife. I like the results so far. When I came to the waves, I decided to put on the music of Jesus Christ Superstar. My oldest son Mark played Pontius Pilot in the play at St. Rocco School. He was young, but for some reason, He projected his voice, Almost as the original actor. I made the mirrored ball that the spotlight shined upon. With music of the finale` trailing off and the lights dimming enough to highlight the mirrored ball. What ever happened to the mirrored ball? Did it go to Dancing with the Stars?

Between the music that moved me. Painting the waves, all the way to the cool fresh sand, and the shining rocky boulders, I felt in another place. In a distant place. Timeless. I painted till three in the morning. But I did not feel tired. I felt at peace, a quiet contentment and gentle elation. The best part was when my sons woke up, upon seeing the almost finished seascape was the wonderment of it all. It was a great way to head off to school. I left a few last details to finish up in class. Upon seeing my painting. Carla exclaimed, "Patti, this is beautiful. How did you achieve the effects? I told her technically, but also told her "By listening to Jesus Christ Superstar." Which was true, the music moved me. The subject inspired me. Sometimes I wonder if there is a gauge to measure the energy level of a finished project or the subject? For subject does matter. John nineteen forty-one: This was the last piece from Jesus Christ SuperStar that would decrescendo into silence. Stillness. A profound sorrow. Very moving...

After I did the seascape, I decided to paint dry land. I found this picture. I loved the sky. The storm coming or the storm breaking. The winds are blowing the grass. I loved the golden colors. This would be the perfect place to again use my palette knives to create the textures of the grasses. The two small buildings in the distance near two small trees. The houses are painted white with red roofs. Move to the forefront surrounded by tall golden grasses are a few wispy trees in front of the—to me it looks like a small church of another time. It is painted white with three added sections to accommodate space needed by the pastor and parishioners. I liked the steeple and the blueish black slate roof. An entry way in the front to greet and meet also provides a gentle protection from the sun, rain, sleet or cold. The roof of the entry way seems to be of a red tile. Complimenting the darker blue slate of the church.

I like the steeple, welcoming and always a presence. There is a small window just before the steeple begins. Behind but near this church are two small houses with red roofs. The tall grasses at one time green, now of rich golden yellows and various shades of burnt umber. Protectively covers the land, the earth. A solitary tree amidst the grasses offering a contrast and purpose that is enduring. The perspective is interesting, it almost has its own story to tell. From season to season. The cycle of life. Doing this painting as if a graceful dance, the swirling clouds to the movement of the grasses in timing and rhythm with the blustering winds. Another study that offers so much.

The dancing grasses. Gracefully moving to the rhythm of the winds. In the distance a few houses or buildings and a peaceful church nearby.

From Painting the forest, to the majestic sea, to the vast grasslands was truly and continues to be valuable lessons learned and appreciated. I was so fortunate to have those few lessons in tole` painting to learn a few techniques and spark that interest to grow a bit further. I have always had an interest in portraiture. One day while leafing through an art book I found the beautiful painting of Irene by Renoir a renowned artist of another time. (early to mid-1800's) "This is what I am going to paint." I proudly exclaimed to Carla Ballaro and my friend Irma Piatoni who was inspired to join this wonderful class. Our subjects were similar in the sense we had both chosen from the great masters. She would do a field scene of a woman—her hair covered with a scarf bent over hard at work. She used the apron of her long skirt to gather the grains that were being harvested. This was the pivotal theme. Interesting but what we chose to do is innate in all of us. Part of who we are, our history wanting to revive, restore and have a greater understanding of who we are. And where we have come from.

    I happily worked on Irene with the beautiful eyes and hair sitting in repose on a bench amongst thick foliage of shades of greens and a suggestion of different shades of florals and varieties in the background. This is a beautiful and resplendent scene of a young girl with beautiful auburn red hair down to her waste. She uses a pretty blue ribbon to pull her hair up off her face. The soft ribbon tied in a bow so soft it drapes down matches her dress. Her hands are gently placed on her lap. A serene and captivating portrait of a young girl probably painted for her family. Would become a beautiful work of art to be displayed and enjoyed throughout Art museums and homes abroad. Here and there.

This is my reproduction of Renoir's Irene. Serene and beautiful.

I enjoyed painting Irene. From the background to her face, and hair to trying to duplicate the folds of her pretty blue dress. I did the best I could at the time I was given. Coincidently, when I found Renoirs' Irene. I found a similar painting titled Precious. I would paint her also. Just to see if I could retain the incentive amid the energy needed with the growing responsibilities that lay ahead. Useful to add to my repertoire of life. Since thoughts of a move were always evident, especially with the kids there was plenty to think about and do. That is why for me it was important that the subject painted was pleasing, worthwhile and inspiring too. I would paint this portraiture also. The style of painting looked so much like a Renoir painting except the name of the artist was different. Yet I have never been able to find the background of the artist. That was not so important to me at the time. But now that I am writing about this portrait, I am rather curious. It was to be the next subject of my painting to compliment the painting of Irene. As before, I would do a quick study and do a light wash of the canvas. Then I would start from the top and work my way down.

There were some differences, the background for one thing. There was a lake and trees behind the standing young girl. The sky looked as if in early evening with a coolness to the air. The lake seemed to have some movement with reflections of the trees and embankment giving depths and interest. Precious, the young girl has her light red hair pulled up at the nape of her neck. A small oval hat of shades of aquamarine and turquoise with small flowers atop like a burst of colorful moss roses. At the base of her hat a soft lavender bow softly drapes her hair. She is looking down at the white daisy in her hands. He loves me. He loves me not. He loves me and he does. How could he not. Around her neck is a sheer scarf that falls and drapes her arms. It must be cool for the cloak around her shoulders, seems of a textured fiber with a few lines down and across. A subtle plaid the colors of deep greens, but mostly blue. There are suggestions of shrubbery in front of Precious painted ever so lightly as being diaphanous. The grasses before the lake has the same diaphanous feel lending a soft aura of mystique. The upsweep of her hair. Soft brush. Soft colors. Genteel. Gentle. A beautiful young girl.

I did another reproduction I call her Precious. A gentle, genteel beautiful young girl.

    I felt a sense of accomplishment doing these few paintings at this time of anticipation and preparation for this big move for our family. But I would also learn I was to have another baby. A baby in August. So, hot time in the summer. We were to take a small trip to the Sand Dunes in Lake Michigan. I bought a one size larger for the bottom part. Maybe two. But I made a top of blue and white checked gingham for the top or bodice. I will try and find the picture of my handy work to show you. It really was simple, but I was at the age of "nothing was impossible to do." Surprisingly, my new bathing suit was perfect for this lighthearted day. We had fun. All of us. The boys would run up the sand dunes. And then, run, slide or roll down the soft sands of the dunes. We would try and make sandcastles before the waves washed them away. Before leaving, we walked along the beach while the waves lapped at our feet. While digging in the soft powdery sand, I was thinking, I'll fill a small container with this wonderful soft sand and do a seascape with the beaches made with a sprinkling of Michigan sand." Making a lasting memory. One Last run of the dunes. And one quick dip in this refreshing lake. Towel off and head for home. A family quick trip. Rick took time. I felt so fortunate. My beautiful, wonderful family.

Shortly after returning home and still inspired, I did paint another big seascape. For the sea is big. Lake Michigan to me is like the sea. I painted the waters. With having a new baby coming soon. I could not dilly dally. I let part of that painting partially dry before I did the rippling of the sand. I took my big canvas out on the front steps of my little red brick bungalow and gently sprinkled the sand from Lake Michigan. I let it dry most of the way. Then when it was ready, I slightly tipped the canvas and let the loose sands free to be part of Ingrid Lane. Now, that was pretty cool. Apropos too. I have heard of people incorporating bits and pieces of nature into their work. This was the first time. And it was sand for me. When your creativity strikes. Try it. Make it fun. Make it funny. Building lasting memories.

Before we moved from Ingrid Lane, Uncle George asked me if I would paint a picture of his son Kenny who played football. It is amazing what you remember. For me that was a pretty tall feat to paint his son in uniform, helmet and all-running across the field. He gave me a small photo, which was rather dark. And, with the helmet on his head, I really could not see his face. It could have been anyone. But Uncle George was pleased with the result. The fact that he trusted me to do this painting was somewhat intimidating for me, I felt such a novice. So, it is amazing what is asked of you and what you can and will do. This was a gift I could give Uncle George and Aunt Lorraine for all they did for our little family. Lessons learned to be able to take that next step. We always learn something of value.

Enjoy and savor those treasured moments, for you never know when added responsibilities appear. My youngest sister moved in with us. Until we moved. We had sold our little burnt red brick bungalow on Ingrid Land and moved the next neighborhood over to Damico Drive—a light tan brick rambler with a nice size yard for the boys. We rented this house for we did not know the date yet of our move. Fortunately, our baby daughter was the most amiable baby. She rarely cried. Her brothers doted upon her. Because of her agreeable nature, she received abundance of attention. I finally had a daughter. When, I almost could not. During this time, I truly felt blessed.

Rick was beginning to think this move was not going to happen. And our temporary lease was up. We bought a pretty cape cod house. Green shutters, the wood stained tan bordered with tan stone. It is a pretty house with a big bay window and carpet of green going up the stairs. Inviting. It was built on a slight hill on a newly wooded lot with a small creek trickling to a stream somewhere. Baby Monica was six months old. By the time my baby girl was eight months old, her brothers taught her to walk. And crawl up the green carpeted stairs.

We had nice neighbors. The neighbor to the left had two young boys. The neighbor to my right was interesting. The husband Tim at one time was a priest and his wife Sarah a former nun. Rick was still traveling to South Bend Indiana. When he was gone for the week, my neighbor, after cutting his grass without a word would quietly cut ours also. I had a small canvas, for some reason I still managed to find a block of time to paint something. I painted a sailboat on the water. But what was unique about this painting was that it was all done with a palette knife. The skies were a summer blue, with shades of pinks and yellows and touches of lavenders and white. The sails picked up the colors of the sky and the waters. The sailboat was of dark brown wood. Thick paint. The waters splashing up to the side of the boat. Shades of blues and greens. I like doing the froth of the waves. All done using oil paints and a pallet-knife. I placed the colors of oil paint I would be using on the pallet board. Using the edge or the tip of the pallet- knife, select the color or colors depending how and where the oil paint would be used using the pallet-knife to apply to the canvas. You can practice different techniques, to discover how to achieve different or the desired effect. This was a fast painting. But fun to do. Because of the thickness, it would take a while for this to dry. But it is worth it and adds another dimension to your repertoire on canvas. Enjoy the experience seeing the contrast. The blending of the colors. How they all work together.

While finishing up this painting, we would learn that we were finally to move. The boys seven and nine. And our baby girl is fourteen months. I liked this house. This little neighborhood that could have been home. We had good neighbors who were considerate and conscientious too. Since the sailboat done with a pallet- knife was still a little wet, I gave this painting to them as a thank you for cutting our grass. When Rick could not be here for his responsibilities we were picking up at work and home for both of us. Since the sailboat painted with a pallet- knife would take longer to dry, I gave them this painting as a thank you. I do not remember what happened to the painting with sand from the dunes. I probably gave my neighbor to the left for their family to enjoy. We had three moves within a year. We would be going to South Bend, Indiana. 17780 Tally Ho Drive.

This move started out a little shaky. Fortunately, Kate and Howard Moody did everything they could to ease this transition. They had a son and daughter about the ages of our boys. Kate knew I painted and introduced me to art programs and instructors. Schools and activities for the kids. Even offering their home as the go to place for meals and laundry. Because our daughter was so young, she adapted beautifully. The Moody's had been here for quite a while and settled in. It felt good to have a familiar face leading the way helpful and welcoming. Once we were settled in our house on Tally Ho Drive, thoughts of the sailboat that I did not bring to our new home, I realized I could duplicate. But it was too soon. I would have to do something different. Grander scale. Challenge myself. I decided I would do this clipper ship.

Off to the left of the kitchen was an eating area, with a functional room divider. One side facing the dining area was a cork board for messages, for events and schedules of activities. This cork board proved to be a very useful apparatus for our family to use. There was also an intercom system to hear if someone was at the front door. The best part, the intercom played music, inside and outside. The patio was half a circle made with burnt red bricks with concrete bordering into a nice sized rectangle with a grill built in the corner. I would notice how the bricks were chiseled to form to the concrete. There was a well thought out fence partially surrounding the two corners with beautiful tall red dahlias tucked in each corner. Creating a semi private but not closed in feel. I liked the two Yucca plants bordering the sliding patio doors. South Bend's weather was a little more moderate than Illinois. But, also in a snowbelt caused by the lake effect when conditions were just right. The winters were not as long but the occasional snowstorms could bring in several feet of snow. But the moderating factor would also come into play and melt the snow away.

One morning, we all slept in. Mysteriously quiet. No electricity but the phone rang. It was my neighbor Kaye, saying, "Patti did you look out your bedroom window?" I had not. But when I pulled up the shade, all I could see was snow. "Oh my gosh." "Patti you have snow up to your roof." My neighbor Kaye is telling me. We had five feet of snow and six to 8 feet drifts. Woke up surrounded by snow. Fortunately, the double doors in the front were sheltered somewhat by the L-shaped wall.

The wonder of it all was, it was not that cold. Just the stillness, the quiet in this wonderful little neighborhood of Carriage Hills. Would take six days to remove the snow from the streets. And four days to remove from our driveway. Only to meet with a wall of snow. When running out of supplies. Rick used the kids' toboggan to take baby Monica, now 2 and ½ years old with her brothers Mark and Duane to the local neighborhood grocery, a mile or so away. Monica surrounded in scarves and soft blankets, wearing her pink and white snowsuit with her little white boots trimmed in white fluff nestled in, perfectly content. Going along on this winter wonderland adventure with her brothers. All were bundled. As I am watching my little family, there was a peacefulness to this whole scene. Almost as a gift. It never got below 32 degrees. Another typical spring snow, but this was extra special. By the time the snow had melted, it felt like summertime.

I found a painting spot that would work best in the breakfast area off from the kitchen. For, to the right was the kitchen area with a small hallway. Going down the hall to the left a laundry room, combination bathroom / mudroom. If the boys came in from that direction, I would see them for I had set up shop in the eating area. To the left of the breakfast area and usually where I would paint would be an inviting family room, with a rust colored shag carpet. I had a great rake to keep the shag pile carpet nice and fluffy. Also, as another form of exercise. Eventually we would get a pretty blue parakeet. We named him Petey. Many times, when I would paint, he would sit on my shoulder. Sometimes, he would gently walk down my arm to get a better picture. He was inquisitive or just wanted some exercise. I usually painted at night when the kids were sleeping. But I remember doing most of this painting in the light of day. As I painted, I faced my easel so I could see the patio, the coming and going of the kids. Monica would be set up on the fluffy rust colored shag carpeting occupied with her favorite toys or scribbles. But she was also a good napper which gave me a routine and the time allotted to do and be. In those blocks of time. I might…

Contemplate what needed to be done as I studied the structure of the ship, there are many parts to a clipper ship like this. Doing the wash and light drawing on the canvas gave me an idea of the intricacies that might lie ahead. Again, I did a light wash. Using a smaller brush, I would put vague lines for the riggings and the masts that support the sails. Behind those masts and numerous sails are rope ladders in there along with the landings. As I am working on the rigging spars and sails, it all started to make sense. I felt the dynamics of the makings of a ship. I could almost feel and hear the bellowing winds against the sails and the deafening sound of the crashing waves striking the bow of the ship. There is no escaping the icy spray or the fierceness of the ocean. And this is just the beginning. But hang on, for land is in the far distance. This was my first painting I did in South Bend to add to my small collection.

This Clipper Ship was the first painting I did when we moved to Carriage Hills in South Bend. A test for myself and would be a special gift.

The sea, lighthouse and the rocky shores intrigued me. Another lesson for me.

    After painting the clipper chip, the sea still pulled at me. I found a picture of a lighthouse on an inlet of a ragged bluff. A storm could be brewing or leaving but looks like a chilly day, nonetheless. I was inspired to paint this channel of water with a lighthouse built on craggy land, a lookout for those lost at sea or needing refuge. An arm of the sea to reach. On that stretch of land grew sturdy but weather- beaten brushes with large boulders to protect whatever land from erosion-- from the sea.

    I worked my way down, from the lighthouse to the grasses and boulders along the shoreline. Then I did the waters, but I was much too eager to do the massive boulders, which of course was done with a pallet-knife. Piles of rocks and boulders with touches of mosses that thrived in the constant moist environment. Tucked between a few boulders would be a few sprigs of spindly growth that would survive the rough elements. The seedlings, "dropped by a bird or critter of some kind" between the rocks finding soil in the most remote and unlikely places. I liked the challenge of doing these rocks and boulders. Lights and darks.

The variations in sizes. Nature has so much to offer. We should always take care, protect and be thankful for our gift of the sea and from the sea.

This was the first time my subject was a pitcher filled with various flowers. Turned to be more of a challenge than I thought. But was well worth it.

After painting seascapes, ships, fields of grasses, forests and streams, I felt a need to try painting flowers. Floral arrangements. The colors were so pretty, the delicate petals, stems and leaves were not as easy as it looked. There certainly was more to this that met the eye. I just wanted to plunge in but for this I needed a certain amount of contemplation and repose with beautiful music playing softly at a distance. I liked the muted colors of the background. The shape of the vase that was the vessel for these pretty flowers within. A variety of flowers with straight sturdy stems of the peony- like rose rising above, the stems that draped down so gracefully tucked in and around with delicate pink flowers and soft almost a gossamer yellow reaching to enhance and frame the bouquet of zinnias. Happy flowers. The golds, a slight rusty red, the subtle changes in the oranges, the pink blending to a light shade of lavender to purple. There is a blue vase with its array of colorful flowers placed on the table—le tableau. The edges of the draped table were softened or muted using a soft brush. Lightly brushing over the edges. A delicate touch to bring out the depths and highlights of the curve of the vase. Take notice to pay attention to the detail. This helps bring awareness in other areas of your life as well.

The poise of this leopard cat captured my attention. He was fun to do and looks great on any wall. Or create a theme that inspires.

This leopard with spots of a regal cat was a nice change of pace. People are drawn to this painting for its stately grace, Also the simplicity of the lines. I did a light wash. Then a general drawing, not too much. For many times painting seems to me, as almost like creating a sculpture. Building on each stroke until the desired shape is formed. After the final stages of this painting, I used a small firm straight brush with a small amount of umber paint, with my finger brushing over the bristles, lightly spray the speckles in the background for an added effect. Actually. A toothbrush works perfectly fine. So, it serves dual purposes. It is always a good idea to practice some techniques to get a feel or touch of how much. Unless this comes naturally. Then lucky you.

Before this time, I did the majestic head of a lion. I brought him to an art exhibition with me. Not to sell, but to inspire. And to give another example of what I have painted. Well, someone liked him as much as I did. Presented an amount that surprised part of me, yet I knew was special. He appreciated and could see the value as much as I. That touched me. I knew I could paint, but what I learned-- there was a process in that transaction. I painted that lion but when I let him go "for a price" that was beyond my expectations. Or maybe I was not ready to let go. Would I be able to duplicate with the same energy, intensity, a certain amount of pride and satisfaction? I should have taken more pictures. But back then our phones did not have that capacity to take photos. And photography was an art. Now it is a lost art, for we all have become photographers, selfies in abundance. Bold and daring. Proper and improper too. Where are the boundaries, the decorum, with grace and respect? At any rate, the painting I would do next would be the Leopard cat. I learned from this painting, not only technique but the emotional energy we put in. It all is important to be able to create with substance, content and with essence in mind. Nonetheless, are we really ready and willing to let go?

Was a pleasant way to start or end my day. Painting a reproduction of Picasso's The Lovers. Simplistic in it's elegance. Universal and timeless in it's story.

    This painting is titled The Lovers. I had to look twice for this was one of Picasso's earlier works. Which I loved. I would duplicate this painting as a reminder for me of so many things in life. The tenderness in the way his arm embraces her shoulders. She is quietly conflicted, uncertain. Yet, her hand clasps his hand in reassurance. There is a beautiful and romantic story in this painting that can unfold in so many ways. Artistes tell their story in visual ways that can be displayed as a memory or event in that certain time. The background painted in a simplistic manner. From the lines of the paned windows painted without a ledge, just straight lines. Even to the gentle curve of the drapes with the subtle touches for the draping.

Just a hint. The colors in the background have only a suggestion of gradation. But it works to bring to the forefront the two lovers. From the boundless olive- green scarf around her hair draping down her shoulders and around her arm. This would be the most intricate part of this painting to bring out the sheerness of the fabric. But, at this point you really want to focus on bringing out that diaphanous or translucent quality of the fabric. Another interesting aspect of this painting, the simplicity also allows the emphasis on the lines to bring out the mood or ambiance to this picture. Almost like a storybook.

Pretty amazing back in those times. The capabilities and workmanship of clothing, draperies, to the craftsmanship of furniture and the structure of buildings, the sales of ships and more. All done by hand with the help of looms for fabrics. Even today, people want to make their own fabrics using looms to make and design their beautiful sweaters, making blankets and rugs too. From threads to yarns. Fibers of all kinds, from the warm wools made from sheep to soft luxurious cashmere to silks and satins. Not only another art form but provides material for our use in life. All is needed and necessary.

From the sublime of Picasso to the subliminal of Van Gough. Van Gough has always been an enigma to me. Someone so talented. Yet so troubled by life. Immersing himself in his paintings to the extreme. As if, wanting to be part of the subject at hand. If only he could immerse himself in his work and bring to life what he could only convey on canvas. Too many times in his frenzy and solitude, he would mistakenly "Or maybe not. Maybe it was his delirium" to taste or ingest the oil paint from his brush, even his palette-knife. That was toxic, especially back then. Eroding his health, his work and quality of life. So, for me, when I found this earlier work of Van Gough, I wanted to reproduce this painting. If only he could have quieted his mind and be in that moment of creating instead of trying to find life through or in his paintings. To be grateful for his talent in the world of art. So, again for me, this will be a tribute to Van Gough from someone unknown in appreciation of his works that still live on. Yet still holds the passion, the mystique and recognition of today.

Why was that or is that? Too many times the struggles are too many. The praise and recognition are left silent as if non-existent until the end. That happens too many times. We do not always need glamour and attention, but appreciation is always needed in some way or some form. Especially when a job is well done and so many will continue to benefit from its lasting treasure.

I decided I was going to try and reproduce Van Goughs' Poppy Fields. This was not a big painting, but it had so much substance and energy that drew me—almost mesmerized. I liked the richness of the colors and texture. Going from the row of houses faintly in the background of slender trees in the distance. Coming to the myriad of poppies in the forefront. To the side there is an old gnarled tree, looks like a trumpet vine with large orange flowers making its way up. I used thick paint on my brush as I worked my way to the forefront. A cluster of red poppies mixed with colors of blue, orange and yellow mix of flowers. Then a plethora of rows of blues, yellows, red and orange colored flowers of different sizes against the dark greens of the stems, leaves and vines. A work of art that could be used in any room. A painting to be treasured for a special someone.

A reproduction of Van Gough's Poppy Field. This painting haunts me, yet delights me--the field of flowers draws me wanting to stay in the moment of gratitude for the beauty that nature offers. Unconditionally, with a little care.

From nature to a mechanical design. I was not so happy with this one. All I could think of were nails and screws. Saws and hammers. Mechanical tubes that shoot out air, currents of electricity even flames, maybe even fumes. There would be filters needed somewhere. Clinchers and pincers to hold tight or pick up tiny objects. I guess I could have designed a car, maybe even a vacuum cleaner. But all I could think of were nails and screws. Until I started the process. This time we could incorporate a color to go with the black ink. Thoughts of blue seemed to be a good color for a machine. But it also could have been a burnt rusty red, shiny silver or brass. But I chose blue. He turned out to be fun to do. Even though more challenging than I thought. Again, with a design once you start it just evolves. Just keep thinking mechanical. And before you know it you have a dancing robot. At least I did. He looks as if he is dancing, prancing off to somewhere. To me, he looks a little formidable with all the clinchers, looks like blades too. But then there are stringed parts, almost like a harp. Maybe, he is trying to decide what he wants to be or do. Actually. He was more fun than trouble.

We were still living in South Bend, Indiana during this time. Our little neighborhood provided something for all my family to flourish in a wholesome environment. Offering diversity in music, the band even plays if their interests were piqued. There were woods with hills and valleys and when the snows came tobogganing, sledding, ice skating, even hockey. There was a special energy to this little town that inspired me quietly. The doors of opportunity at almost every turn. Education for one. Forever not too far, a hop skip and a jump from Notre Dame. The beautiful campus pulled at me, drew me in. Then there was St. Marys' College in its serene setting. Toward the end of town there was IUSB Indiana University of South Bend. Where I decided to enroll for classes. Not as a fulltime student for I was married with children. I had responsibilities that could not be ignored. Yet, the doors of opportunities were awakening possibilities.

There always is a way. Back then, education was affordable. The only issue for me was time. Depending on the class I would take two or three classes a semester. To encourage and as an impetus for myself, I would take another form of art class. To be well rounded. That is when I was introduced to Harold Zissla a master, "I say" or professor of design and creative design. I took both. Not at the same time, as I had my literature, history and social studies, a psychology course to understand myself and others too. What drives us. Why we do the things we do. I would learn these areas of life to prepare myself for when the unexpected in life showed up to be prepared. I took a few business classes for that really is being responsible. I felt I should be responsible and capable and a bit more knowledgeable too. Again, more rounded also.

After that first year I took a drawing class from Alan Larkin, even a small stint of life drawing. I drew objects I never would have never been inspired to draw. But surprisingly in a classroom structure you draw the seemingly impossible. And for some reason find yourself immersed in that study. Taking a drawing class trains your eye to see the curve, straight lines to the angles, the shading, the darks and lights, the dimension and distance. Helps in so many aspects of life. I enjoyed these classes and was surprised to learn when taught with real interest, intent and understanding the reason and purpose even the rationale. You want to learn more. Sometimes even a little humor can draw you in keenly. The love of learning never ends.

Therefore, from the Poppy Fields of Van Gaugh to the painting of Picasso's The Lovers, I would go into a design classroom structure. That proved to be exciting for me. At first Harold Zissla was not happy with me. For I missed the first week. But there was a reason for that. These classes started a week earlier than for my kids. My children were my main priority. I knew what I could do, but it was important this new routine was established smoothly for all of us. So, when I walked in the classroom that first day for me, he turned to me and said I should leave and get my money back. I was shocked. When I explained my situation. He said, "if you think you can catch up. Then stay." And I did. What a way to start my first day. Yet I knew what I could do in class. And I also knew the importance of my family. I would not think of having my children start the school year alone at home. Taking these classes were to enhance not only my own life, but for my family also. Whatever we do, we do for a healthy reason and purpose that enhances life. Learning new skills keeps your mind sharp. That is what I learned in design. Starting a project. The unknown. The developing of ideas, how to implement and relax and let the inspiration flow.

The design from nature was for my first class for Harold Zissla. Awakening of ideas.

My first real project in design class would be to create a design from nature. I liked nature so that was a good thing for me. For some reason, my first design became a Nature from the Sea. Well it could have started out with squirrels, foxes, owls in a tree and deer in a lush forest of trees, wildflowers amidst greeneries. This was done with pen and ink. So, once you start, let it go. Let it flow and enjoy the process of designing something new to you. Unique. I must have been thinking of sea life. For, before I knew it, this design had a life of its' own. Seemed as if, in a body of water in the depth. Organisms part of nature in the waters. Undisturbed, but there is a purpose. Water plants gracefully flowing to the light ripples of water as if in a graceful dance itself. There seems to be a tail of a fish forging its' way down and through. Star fish, tendrils and tentacles wispy and delicately adding to the foray of the waters. Maybe an Octopus reaching up with his arm of tentacles. Searching. Whatever for. Let your imagination flow to places you have never seen before. Design from nature. Harold Zisslas' design class.

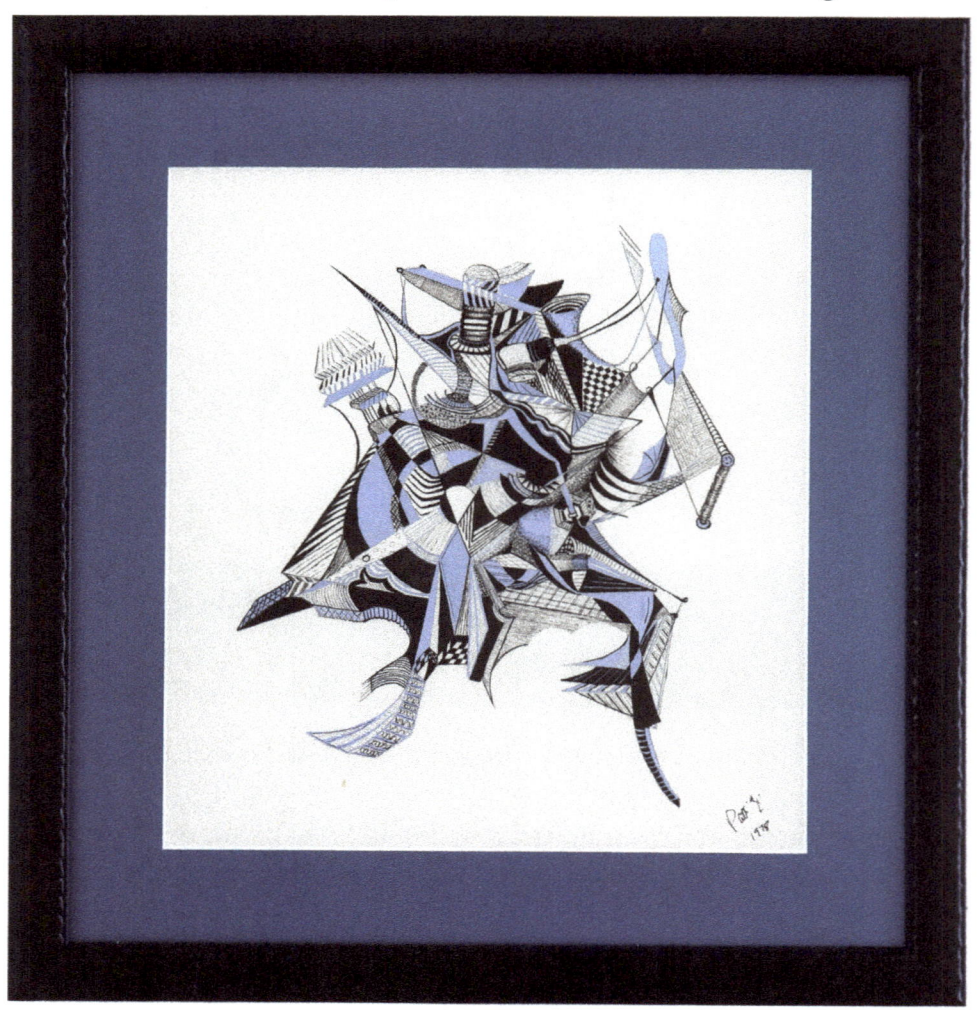

Mechanical design in Harold Zissla's class. This design was great fun to do. Whimsical and challenging at the same time.

This was the last design I did in this segment. Would like to do another.

We were to do three designs. Design from nature, mechanical design and the last a design from ornamentation. Well, I was looking forward to doing this one. For this design, I was thinking of course jewelry, tapestry, quilts, and fabric designs. Maybe, I had too many ideas, for instance adding fringe, a painted fingernail, a dove, a rose, an acorn. Incorporating symbolism in this design, the tree of life, a butterfly' wing, the last apple on a limb, a cross symbol of faith. For some reason, this design was more of a struggle. Maybe, it was because I had too many options. At any rate, what was interesting was the fact that all these designs had a quality of movement to them. During this time, I was taking ballet and jazz which subconsciously became part of my work. Designs are fun to do. Can be intricate to simply elegant. Having a theme helps form your ideas or plan for your next design.

An interesting thing, shortly after I did this design as I opened my computer a sailboat came on my screen. Reminding me of my sailboat I had done completely with a pallet-knife and gave to my helpful neighbor. There was a difference. This sailboat was longer. Made with dark wood, as mine. But the sails were square and larger. Colorful and magnificent. The sails were made from different patchworks, as a quilt. The patches on the sales were cheerful. Would be a welcoming and inviting change from the ordinary, but extraordinary still, on the open waters. There were patches of all kinds that worked together. An olive branch, a dove, a gold star and more but the placement of one patch that stood out was simple. All white but in the center a large red heart. Can you imagine the goodwill and joy that would inspire just being, just seeing this incredible display made to brighten the days? For me it was serendipitous and encouraging too. Let this be for you.

The nature, mechanical and ornamentation designs were from the first semester with Harold Zissla. I learned so much. Always inspired. I definitely wanted to see what the next semester would bring. Another interesting observation through this process of creativity, the effect going into the classrooms of my more serious subject, I should say worthwhile or practical even necessary-- really did enhance all those classes. I was more willing and ready to expand my knowledge in other areas of life. I wanted to live life—capable and contributing. We all can do that. I was fortunate that I had reason and purpose that propelled and motivated me. We would do three big projects. I caught my breath when I learned about our next assignment. Could I do it? The excitement of the challenge started to simmer within me. Subject, color ideas coming to surface. This was going to be another great undertaking…

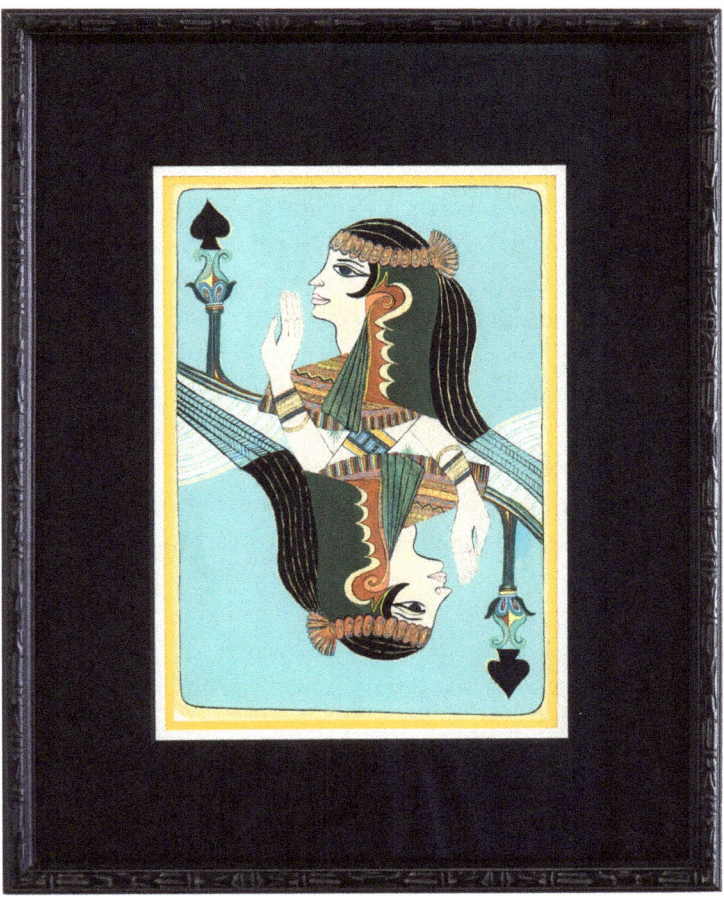

I decided to do a queen of spades to be done freehand. Which was really challenging. Concentration and focus is needed. The first one I did I call her the daughter Queen of Spades. In shades of aqua. reds and golds.

    I would learn we were all to design our own face card. I decided I would design the Queen. Queen of Spades. Getting to match or duplicate the top and bottom was the most challenging. Coordinating the features was a little tricky. But not impossible. Just needed patience, a block of time without too many distractions. And encouragement is always helpful. I had to do two face cards. Similar. But different colors. I had to use a few measuring tools in the beginning, but once the painting began, I was on my own with my paints and brushes needed. I was always intrigued by Egyptian history, folklore, the pyramids with the majestic mystique of its traditions. The pageantry in their "pomp and circumstance."

Once my decision was made, I chose my colors of aquamarine, greens, some blues and rusty tones with ambers and golds. On my palette I would also need whites, shade of red—maybe some yellow. Just a tad to blend for the queen of spades skin and might use touches throughout. Some black to out line and for her hair and I am ready to begin. This also needed concentration and a steady hand. I painted the large areas first and then added the embellishments. Her hair, then the headdress and cloak to the bracelets around her wrists and arm. It all needs a little thought for ideas to flourish and then flows to come together. Because this was all done by hand, there are some irregularities. But to me, just add to the charm and acceptance. Good enough. I had another one to do. Plus, my family to attend too.

Next Queen of Spades was a bit more challenging. Maybe it was because it was too close to the first. And, I do not have the heart for repetition. Or maybe, it was the color I chose. I chose pinks and blues. Which never felt Egyptian to me. One day, while looking at my display I decided to change and rearrange this particular graphic design face card. I had way too many things going on, so this was not my best idea. (I was living in my little cottage house at this time) As not to see the pink, I covered the entire front with burnt golden paint. Now I decided the colors would be golds, purple, reds with touches of blue. Before this, I gently used some fine sandpaper to soften the picture. I felt a certain remorse doing this. But could not turn back now.

This would already have a different feeling. I referred to this Queen of Spade, not her sister, but her mother even grand-mere. She has been through so much. Life has not been gentle for her. Sometimes not even kind. Yet, has a certain strength, sapience and courage to endure and persevere. For she has learned her reason and purpose. I chose deeper colors for her. Purples and reds, but I added vines with leaves and flowers even a heart in there, to surround her. This face card has an aged look, for all the layers of paint applied to conceal the beginning. But she is regal. She prefers to be cloistered surrounded by nature and those she loves from a distance. Independent. Yet, knowing she is protected by the Universe.

Note* I tried to keep in sequence, my paintings, and designs. But upon writing this, life changes. I moved back to Edina. I hung this painting above the door in my little office—stocked with artifacts, bulletin boards, a picture of Jesus on the bulletin board and a paper machete butterfly Melissa made for me.

Every thing of inspiration and the most necessities needed in an office. I have paintings, photos of all kind, a wise owl, even angels climbing the corner wall. I bought them at Ten Thousand Villages when I did volunteer work there. I have art books, a big antique dictionary, some files, my standing writing desk, an oriental secretary desk, two bookcases. It all fits. As if I have my own museum of interests. It is also my creative space for inspiration and ideas flourishing to fruition. I also have a framed print given to me of a tennis bear holding a tennis racquet. He is cute, wearing his white tennis shoes, his Wimbledon white tennis shirt and shorts with a white visor to shield his eyes from the sun. He is ready to play. First serve, love-love. Let's Go.

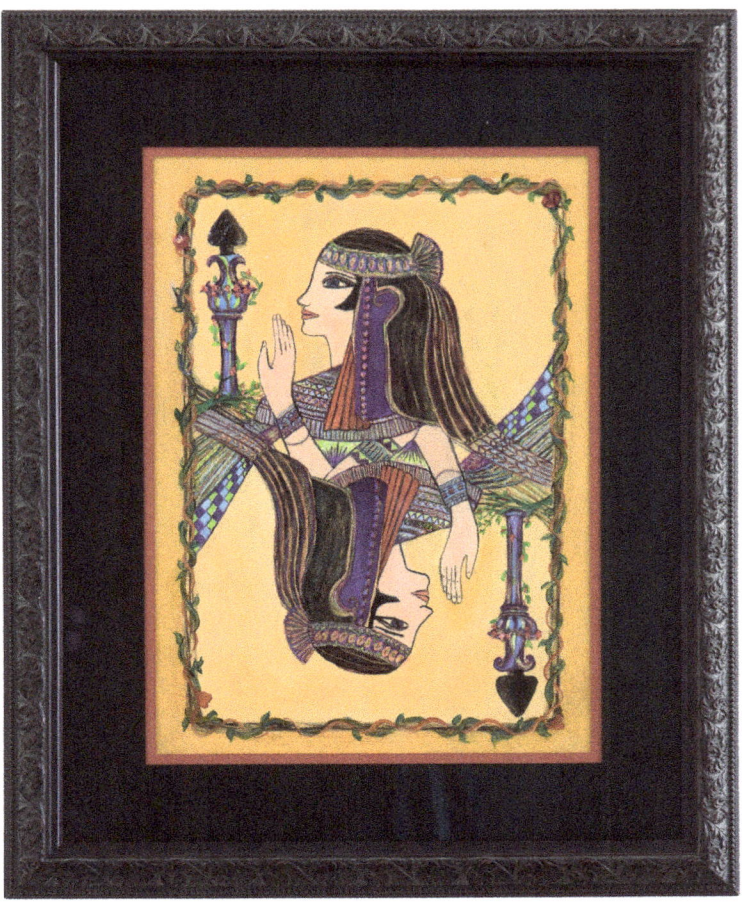

The second face card design I decided to do the Mother Queen of Spades. In colors of purples, shades of reds and golds. Surrounded by vines.

I already did the writing for these two face cards. Actually it was quite elaborate, so I hope you enjoy them.

****

Michelangelo 1475-1564

After designing the face cards, we were to do a graphic design of a known historical figure and add a quote that might be appropriate. I was taking an Art History class during this time and felt Michelangelo would be the obvious choice. I happen to have a plaque "We Never Stop Learning" underneath Michelangelo's name. That is what I believe also. To me that is exciting. But that is not the quote I used. In my graphic design, I had put "Art is difficult. Transient is its' reward" by Shiller. Why in the world did I even put that? I guess because we are always on to the next challenge. Be it creatively, musically, athletically, and professionally. Sometimes it is our own expectations. Or the expectations from others, whom we try not to disappoint.

I was fascinated by Michelangelo. His versatility and capabilities. He knew what he could achieve and that was perfection. He expected the same from others. But everyone has their own style in their own time to learn and understand. The ability to be able to trust and work together. The great artists impressed me Renoir, Monet, Van Gough and many more. And of-course Michelangelo.

Later I would have the opportunity to travel to Rome, Italy. While I was in Rome, I would visit the Sistine Chapel. The history in this time was fascinating. Sometimes spellbinding. For during this time, Rome was the Mecca for artists, composers, musicians, writers, scholars, and poets. All appreciated and valued. Being the perfectionist that Michelangelo was, he preferred to do the ceilings himself. Yet, the task was so monumental the impatience grew amongst Cardinal Giovanni, the patrons and those wanting to be involved, insisted local artistes help paint the Sistine Chapel. This project would take years anyway. Michelangelo eventually relented, but his pride was deeply hurt. During this Michelangelo had worked himself into such a creative passion he felt, "he alone was capable." He probably was, but he was just one man. Now working with all the other artists, all the commotion, the different styles of work taking shape and form was like a giant cartoon to him. Michelangelo wanted perfection. To him, the ceilings were becoming like a cartoon. In his rage, when the artists were done for the day, Michelangelo locked and bolted the doors. He would not let them in. When they returned the next day, and the next day after that. Michelangelo still would not let them in to continue their work. They beat on the doors. Yelling for Michelangelo to let them in. Well, he was high on his scaffold redoing to his satisfaction. Thankfully, he could not hear for his deep concentration and being far removed.

There is so much more to this historical event and time. To my flight back home, from my incredible trip to Italy. Michelangelo was so much on my mind. On my flight back, I started reading the condensed version of Michelangelo's life. We had a four-hour layover in Holland. The airport there was beautiful, superior, like a vacation itself with lovely comfortable seating areas. I went to get a bite to eat along with the long line of passengers. As I am waiting, there was a tall interesting looking gentleman behind me. We started talking. I told him he looked familiar. Not that I knew him. Yet, from somewhere. He told me his name. Ronny Woods. He then handed me his card for he is also an artist and musician. Played with the Rolling Stones. He was polite and gracious. What a wonderful way to end this trip. This brief unexpected encounter was the perfect ending to this trip. From the artistic world. To the world of musicians. A gift to all.

But there was still more to come. This flight had the most comfortable seating. Now, I can never sleep on a plane, but these seats were spacious and plush. What a wonderful treat. I nestled in my comfortable seat and opened my book, thinking I would probably fall asleep for sure. But that did not happen. I am contentedly reading, as Michelangelo is feverishly working on this tremendous ceiling before him. Stretching to reach here and there. To the highest points to the tightest spots even laying on the scaffold to get to the low- lying areas. He is working so passionately on the Sistine Chapel. How could I possibly sleep? I wanted to do something to help. I could feel his determination I felt as if I were painting along with him. I could not sleep with Michelangelo working so hard and so long. I wanted to help Michelangelo, even if vicariously. As I am reading, I felt I was there. I never slept a wink, until the flight touched down. Then it was too late for me. The glory of it all.

Well, Michelangelo would be my last project for Harold Zissla in graphic art design. I decided to do a bust of Michelangelo. We were to work with three colors. Since this was taken from a bust, a sculpture of the head of Michelangelo-- I used the colors black, taupe, and white with real gold paint mixed in for a sheen. He has a very intense face, with great character and a nice Roman nose. Because of his thick curly beard and his mustache turned slightly down past his lower lip, this was an interesting project. His eye- brows are thick accentuating the intensity of his piercing eyes. He has a well- shaped head with thick curly hair, that grows down to his beard. He is a handsome powerful man. A genius in his work. A master of his calling. He signed his name in Italian. I liked the way he did that.

The reason I chose the quote, "Art is difficult. Transient is its' reward." I believe we are always searching. We have our successes, but also the pull of another challenge. It is not difficult to bask in your glory. But you do not want to linger. But appreciate the gifts we have before us. For, we are always learning. That is what keeps us vibrant. Giving us reason and purpose.

Michelangelo.
I chose to do the bust or head of Michelangelo for my last graphic art design class.

Going into summer break, I was told, Jim Borden was offering a few portraiture classes using live models. Just the head or bust. There were just a few classes. This is also where I met Janice Woods. We were in the same portraiture class. We had similar interests. We laughed when we learned we had so many. Of course, we became good friends. Sympatico, we were. We met in an art class, but also had the love of tennis and our philosophy on life and importance of family. We both had daughters named Monica. The difference, she had two daughters and a son. And, I had two sons and a daughter. Serendipitous, this meeting would be. Janice took this oil painting class…

But she preferred doing watercolors. And when we moved once more, we exchanged paintings. Janice gave me a snow- covered mountain scene with valleys of thick snow. In the snow- covered valley, there are dried brushes peeking through the snow. To the left are a smattering of tall pine trees with fresh fallen snow captured in the boughs of the pines. From the base of the pines there are clumps of snow and wisps of grasses throughout. There must be a narrow path for on both sides there is sparse dried grass on each side. To the right of the path there are indications of trees displaying rows with reddish pink leaves. The wispy trees are almost lost in the blowing snow. To the far right there are more pines, with touches of fresh fallen snow. For the snow on the mountains thick with tops of pines way in the distance forging through the snow. The ridges and valleys are portrayed by using shadows and shades of darks and lights with just a light touch. The sky is cloud covered with hints of the lightest of greys and softest touch of blues. With just a tad of the lightest pinks. You will have to look closely. What a wonderful gift of remembrance.

I have that painting in the master bedroom over a chair of tapestry. I gave Janice a picture of wild daisies in a vase, the canvas was oval, which is unusual. We both still have these special paintings. But, where you live, the things you do and the time of life. Are all significant. Writing about this first portraiture brought back memories of dear friends once more. Memory lane.

* *

Portraiture of a young man with thick curly hair. This was a one class project.

    This portrait of a young man with thick curly hair was one of my projects in Jim Borden's one-time portraiture class. I also did the young woman in pink.
    There was a smattering of students eager to begin a portraiture, maybe some valuable technique or insight from Jim Borden. What could he teach them that they could not see themselves? How to trust what you see for one thing. To be a little fearless for we all make mistakes. That is how we learn. The form for another thing. The lines, how they curve, the shading or the subtle shadows for doing a face or a figure is never one dimensional or flat. This would be a one-day class. Therefore, we had to do this subject quickly. For the next day there would be a different model. Sitting for this first day was a young man with thick dark curly hair and dark eyes. He displayed a somber expression as if, this was a temporary part of his learning experience. I was disappointed that we would

not be able to finish that day. When we had a small break, I would check to see if any of the other budding artists subconsciously painted something of themselves in their portrait. Subconsciously of course. Ironically, it seemed to be. Some more prominent than others, but it is something that happens. We leave part of ourselves in the work we do.

Young man my first portraiture with Jim Borden.

A young woman with long pink scarf.

Young woman in pink in another time.

Our next class would be a young woman with a pink scarf wrapped around her head. The pink scarf was long enough that it drapes across her right shoulder. She had shoulder length blond hair, with a few golden strands of hair peeking out from her scarf. She is in deep thought. The left side of her shoulder shows a hint of her light turquoise blue sweater. It was interesting to paint the scarf that accented the features of her face. Her hair escaping from the scarf is an added interest. Because this was another class that was to be done quickly. Everyone did a quick wash of the portraiture. Just a few minutes left, but not enough time to finish what we started. We all walked out with our incomplete painting.

That is why, these two paintings do look incomplete, for they are. These two paintings are done on canvas boards. That is part of my reason. I prefer the surface of stretched canvas on a wooden frame. One of these days, I will be inspired to restore these two paintings. I do not like projects that are left incomplete. It pulls at me even after many years. But everything well done happens in its own good time. These designs and paintings were done when we first moved to South Bend, Indiana the home of Notre Dame and St. Mary's. We would learn we would be uprooted once more. We would leave behind incredible friends but never far from my heart or thoughts. We would have those lasting memories that might fade but are always near and dear to our thoughts. Never forgotten.

⁎⁎⁎

Minnesota

Now we would be moving to Minnesota. A week before Christmas. I wonder whose Idea that was. Some things we prefer to forget, but then we would never really understand. The cause and effect. Our sons were young teenagers. Our daughter is too young to remember or understand. They needed reassurance that this was the right place to be. I did too. Would this unite us as a family or divide us? Would there be quality time or would we be spread too thin. Not enough time. Not any time. Corporate America divides us. For their bottom line is the main priority at whatever costs. We should know. So, we could be prepared. Not left in the dark. Not left to struggle. It all sounded so wonderful. But it was just to entice. It was not right. But the rewards would be too great. But one would prosper. Move on without a thought. No looking back.

Now we have opened the Pandora box and cannot even begin to unravel the mess, or pick up the chaos, for the unreachable egos get in the way. Not wanting to remember their part of the disgrace of what was done to our human race. Why can't we get this right? Why we have not learned those too many lessons. It is a mystery to me. Inconceivable to me, that we continue moving backward. Not for better but to manipulate in their favor. What happened to our conscience, accountability, responsibility? Our sisters and brothers. Fathers and mothers. We come in all colors. We are all the same. Why can't we see the damage that we have done? That we continue to do. For we still have not learned. Ignorance and its followers. We cannot accept indifference any longer. Wake up from your slumber. Start anew for me and you. Start small. Let your numbers grow to inspire each other. Awaken to your gifts that God has given. The Universe will thank you when we take care of each other. We can do that. But I have to tell you...

This move still took its toll. For the stakes were too high. The price was the sacrifice. You cannot erase that. Or pretend it didn't happen. Or did not matter. Or worse than that, it was not that important. There is always a cause and effect. Lives have changed and not for the better. Whenever experiencing inequity or indifference without being heard for understanding. There will continue to be struggles, until we stop profiting off the mistakes that have been made and perpetuated through neglect. There needs to be responsibility and accountability. If that is not possible, then hang up the towel. For are they deserving or even capable?

Designer rules were set up to profit—someone. Or for an agenda to serve their own purpose. I could feel the difference in structure. What was it? Control. Maybe controlling. Or was it controlling the situation. The trade off, was it even acceptable? Time would tell, sometimes immediately but we must not have been listening. Maybe, it was the wording, the transcript that we didn't quite understand. I made an appointment to check out the Art School here. The art was more modern. There were some interesting pieces but nothing that inspired me. Plus, they wanted me to take a full load. We just moved here. I could not justify that kind of commitment for my kids going through the same changes as me. Plus, I am their mother. They would need me. My husband would need me also. I could not be working on paintings when we all were trying to find our way-- to make this our home.

The music was different in the band. My ballet and jazz did not have the same feel. I could not find any artist friends to relate to. Woe is me. Winters are the longest month in Minnesota. There was Northwest Racquet Club which we would join. Now that took skill and commitment. There went my creative endeavors. Although, I did join the Edina Chorale and that was wonderful. The kids were going through their transition, which proved to be more challenging than either one of us imagined. And my husband was impressing those in his firm. But never enough time for family anymore. We tried to make it work for years. But Corporate America always takes more than it gives.

A quick painting near Lake of the Isles. A shaded area on a hot summer day.

On the hottest day of the summer, my friend Joyce and her art instructor came from St. Paul to Minneapolis to paint the Lake of the Isles scenery. Hopefully the lake, but it was so hot we had to find a shady spot. We found a shaded glen nearby, did a wash very quickly. I did a few embellishments but left the rest for later. I had this small unfinished painting done on a canvas board tucked in a corner shelf. Even though it wasn't quite finished, it still had a certain charm. I eventually had him framed to give him dignity and to correct his alignment. He's in my office right now.

I would not have the block of time needed or the focus for challenging works now. My friend Jill introduced me to Joyce, an aspiring artist friend of hers. She insisted I keep painting. One sweltering summer day, in the upper 90's, she brought easels, an assortment of brushes, oil paints and a palette for each. She also brought her instructor John. We all were all going to the lake of the Isles to paint. It was not far from my house, but because of the weather we drove. We walked around looking for the perfect spot, but so hot, even the gentle breeze left no relief. There was a grove of trees with worn grass for a path near Lake of the isles. Somewhat, secluded. With a lot of shade but the air stifling still.

We started setting up on our desired spot. This was as good as it was going to get on this hot day in the summertime. Joyce was spreading a blanket on the grass and set up her easel nearby. I was thankful, my canvas board was so small. I did my quick wash, then added my sliver of sky and the cluster of trees in the summer breeze. Added some tall grasses, with a smattering of lilies—I do believe. There was a hint of blue sky, but not of water. It was too hot to even talk. Just do what we were determined to do. The bright sun made the leaves sparkle. I finished what I had to do. John looked at me and said he did too. We looked behind us to see how Joyce was doing. She was asleep on the blanket. She is no dummy. We looked at her canvas, a few lines here and there. The heat must have really gotten to her. But still I have this first picture done in Minnesota as a reminder of this very hot day. And my new friend who cared enough to recognize the importance of doing what we love. Patti Z. not quite complete. Complet; completer

****

Going back in time—Drawing charcoal etc.

I remembered taking another art class from Alan Larkin. We were asked to bring a large pad of plain newspaper for we were going to draw. We were to bring drawing pencils, charcoal pencils, and soft pastels. Artist Chalk that has a fine consistency for fine work. I would have all these supplies for life. I was excited about this class. Until…

Alan Larkin came into the room so proud of himself, carrying a big bag with lots of stuff inside. Out poured a hodgepodge plus a mix bag of the most uninspiring junk, I would say. A real old bone, even an animal skull bone. Where in the world, did he find these things? Each bag seemed to have a theme. Another bag might have tools or even part of a tool, screws, bolts various things you would find in a toolbox. Lost and now found. And the other bag, out came wrinkled fabric, a crumpled paper bag, colorful folded fabric, threading needles and pins, with spools of thread. So interesting. Scissors, a cup and broken cup, even some dried flowers. Take your pick. All meant to teach us something. What started out as questionable turned out to be a great teaching tool. All the contraptions, gadgets and gizmos, utensils of all kinds were displayed. We selected our subjects and began our creative endeavor.

We also would Practice drawing our own hand, a foot, a shoe and an old sock strewn on the floor. All were challenging and surprising with interesting results. The items I chose, I tried to coordinate in a pleasing manner. Some were more practical, pragmatic. Just getting these things done and nothing more. After all, what would we ever do with these drawings? But life has a way that surprises us, even amazes us. To think, we might use these drawings one day to put in our laundry room, our workshop, our garage even in our toolbox. A reminder of our creative life once upon a time. What we learn and how we learn carries with us throughout our life. One more acquired conquest to add to our repertoire of life.

Rummaging through my portfolios filled with past drawings, I found my charcoal drawings where we had to blacken the papers with charcoal and do a still life using an eraser. Now, that was challenging but teaches to see the lights and dark in a different way. So, to be more observant. To preserve the finished piece, lightly spray with a fixative. Allow yourself time, when working on a special project. For time goes quickly without realizing it. You can become so absorbed in your work, before you know it, time is over. This is your special time. And, if it is a family project you're working on, you want to enjoy the experience. So, prepare and plan this time. Have fun and be as creative and adventurous as you dare.

Practice of drawing our own hand in Alan Larkin's drawing class.

Drawings of the hand is a great study. And also, is what is required in art school. Your own hand is a perfect place to begin. But, before you begin I want to tell you about the famous artist Albrecht Durer. A famous artist from 1471 to 1528. He came from a large family, very poor. Not enough money to send two talented sons to art school. So, the two brothers tossed a coin. It was Albrechts lucky break, for the coin fell in his favor. His brother would work in the mines to help support their family. Albrecht Durer forever felt torn. To honor his brother, he would one day draw his brother's hands that were evident of all his years of hard labour and his sacrifice. Drawn and finished down to the very last detail were his brothers' hands. How could he show his deep gratitude? The Praying Hands became world wide famous.

Random objects place on a table outside.

Soft brown pencil drawing of various of objects of interest.

This was drawn with a reddish brown charcoal pencil. There had to have some sheen coming from various objects, a light source and of course there would be shadows. We used brown paper, to an inexpensive newspaper without print. It is obvious, I'm not a Michelangelo or Duerr. But, you can be, if you choose your own unique style.

Little Cottage House

When I sold my condo, I bought a little cottage house. It needed a lot of work. More than I was prepared for. But this little house, as challenging as it was, became a labor of love in the end. I never forgot my first lion that I had accidently sold. For he was beautiful, from his grand mane to his majestic carriage and aura he presented. For he was a majestic lion. I had a canvas. And I was recovering from a long illness. This is what I needed after all these years. To recapture my captivating lion. When I was at the Chicago Lincoln Zoo, I could see a beautiful lion resting on a large quarry stone. He was from a distance, and there was a thick wire fence between us. I took a picture with my little camera. I found that picture and started painting him in my return to a healthy me. There is always a reason why things are not as they should be.

At this stage, life shifted dramatically for all of us. For one thing, the kids were grown with responsibilities of their own. Of course, as parents we still had our duties and obligations to fulfill. But how could we be the best that we could possibly be, when we were submerged in legalities meant not to bring understanding and dignity to the forefront. But meant to prolong and drain the mind, body and soul, the resources too. How could this happen or be allowed to happen? When in the beginning and during we complimented each other. Our differences complimented. Successes too many. Instead of being content and thankful. We became the pawn for somebody else's ideals. To win. Take over. Always a sacrifice for the right price was acceptable. The eschewed values replaced human value. Replaced love and understanding; We all have our own stories to tell. Living in the time of disconnect and indifference.

The further I go into my artbook, a timeline of events, the memories can't help but come along. I painted this new lion back then, as a tribute to the lion that was senselessly slain. This lion was aged, prized, and protected. Yet, because of ego and a dream to fulfill, he was allowed. That seems to be the way it is now, more than ever. And some people still can't understand the magnitude of such actions. It had been almost a year with this illness and still lingered. For so long. That this recovery would not happen overnight. It would be a process. I decided to paint my lion intermittently. In my well time and rest and take care when needed. Painting did take my mind off my physical self. In the process, I felt a sense of normalcy, another day, and a creative way to restore and heal. Soon. Hopefully.

Everyday that I painted on my lion, I enjoyed it immensely. But the closer I came to the final touches. I could not seem to get there. This was a gentle lion. Almost with human features. In fact, he was a sweet lion. I tried to paint him with some fierce qualities or more of a commanding presence, but he stayed docile. He did not want to go there in the wild yet. He was not prepared. He just wanted to be admired for his difference. And appreciated. So, I accepted that. I had a check up recently with my doctor. I was telling him the history of trying to reproduce my first lion. He is a wise man. He said, "Well maybe there is a reason for that." And I believe so. It is time that we bring our values back. Our virtues—love and kindness. To find our moral compass and bring back goodness, and our moral excellence. We can learn from each other when we bring out our best.

Well that picture was not the clearest. But, probably more so, the fact I still was on the mend. I forgot how the eyes of this lion was, his nose including his jaws. He looks battle worn. Weary. Too tired to hold his position of king of the jungle. But he is well liked.

Yes, I would try and duplicate my majestic painting I did years ago. But, had nothing to compare to, except a faint photograph and from a distance. I still liked him. He was different. He definitely had some human features. Maybe, this was the delirium of my illness. One of these days, I will fix him. For he is on canvas and patiently waiting. People have given me growling, prowling, stalking cats, but I just don't have the heart to change him. Yet.

This was when I was living in my little cottage house. I bought this string of angels when I was doing some volunteer work at Ten Thousand Villages. I saw these little angels on a string. I bought them and put them in my office. Always as a reminder of angels watch over us.

For the placement is over the fireplace in my little cottage house, which is over a 100 years old. On the ledge is a wooden putter from Scotland. Next to the Scottish putter is a brass candle snuffer. The lower part of the fireplace is aged brick with dark wood, with ornate engravings. Antique. Priceless to many. Precious to some.

Little Cottage House, painting to heal

While I was doing volunteer work at Ten Thousand Villages, I found these little handmade falling or climbing angels on a sturdy fine cord. Just busily trying to come down, or trying to find their way up. They are really sweet. One of these days will be a very special gift. For someone.

Four complete birdhouses. Lucia, Vince and Zoe had painted on craft day.

My brother Billy gave this Lion a name of Judah.
He has had many names too, Leo, Cleo, Lucky and Ella. He is a friendly Lion.

The five foot head of King Tut.
To save expenses, these mural were done on large rolls of brown paper,
using house paint. When finished, taped to the designated wall.

Sarcophagus is singular. Sarcophagi is plural. I had painted 3 sarcophagi a mother, son and daughter and 5' head of King Tut Painted the message wall for Monica's graduation.

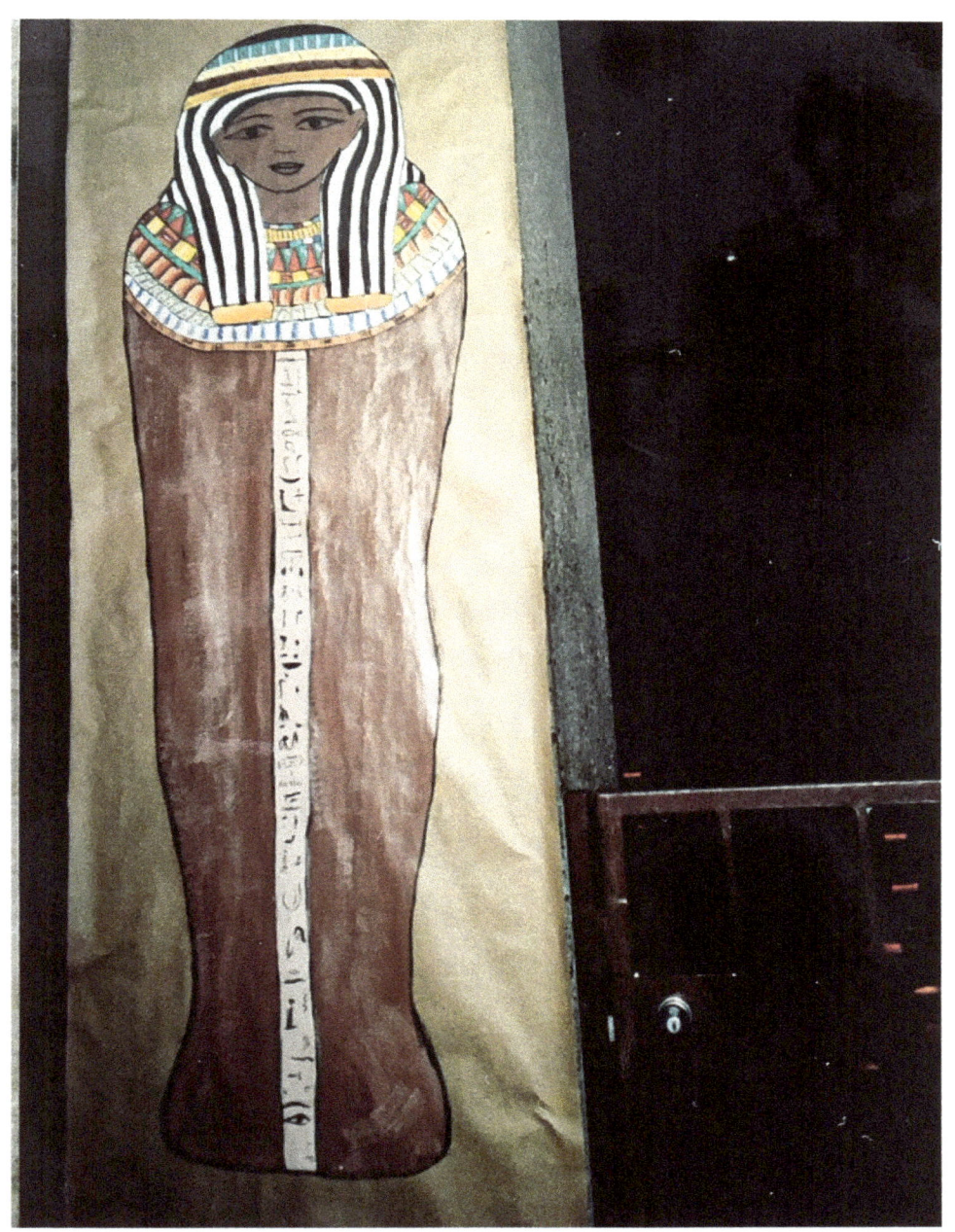

The Young Boy Sarcophagus

The Young Girl Sarcophagus

Jackie, Me and Edie taking a break at our daughters' graduation party outside my house.

Friends and classmates at graduation party in the backyard and Mill Pond.

Continuation of graduation party.

Charcoal drawing of pottery. And aloe plant in a square clay pot.

    I have come to the final pages of my art book. My hopes that this book is filled with inspiration for you, bringing an awakening of possibilities that you never knew possible. I know for myself, I did have an inkling of what came naturally for me. For I grew up as an inquisitive child filled with wonder and curiosity. That never went away. Became part of who I was. I loved music. I loved dance, in those quiet spaces of times I might be drawing--something. But, most of all I felt these abilities and many said talents were a gift to me. So, I was thankful. These gifts would help me throughout life, guide me and direct me to what came naturally. Family, friends and teachers who noticed or recognized and encouraged these gifts in me, helped bring me out of my shell to build confidence and expand my dreams and interests. we all have been given unique abilities. All we have to do is be receptive and healthy, in mind, body and spirit.

Different designs with needle and thread in Alan Larkins' class.

    Because of the pandemic, writing this book presented so many conflicting emotions. In the beginning, my writing acted as a buffer. Taking me away to a comforting and pleasant time, where I wanted to be. To stay. To go back. But, of course that was impossible. My painting evolved as well as our family with each move. There was a dramatic change. Our last move would be a corporate move. Our children were growing up. Monica was still pretty young, but our sons were going in their teens. The Corporate world takes charge, demands and entices. Portrays and presents the offer too good to refuse. But, only presented one side of the picture. Not the reality of life when being uprooted from friends, family, the familiar to the unknown. And, to this day. We are all still here. But, not together. That is too high a price.

This book was like a giant timeline for me. from Chicago, to South Bend to Minnesota a week before Christmas. How can you forget? In Minnesota, winters came quickly and is the longest season. That takes some getting used to. Most Minnesotans had their cabins up north in the summer. And their winter place in Florida, Arizona someplace nice and warm. Maybe even exotic. But our house was also our vacation home, for my husband was so dedicated to his work. But, he would take Spring Break with everyone else. A week was never long enough. Minnesota loves their sports, and fishing openings come on Mothers Day here. Easter, there is usually snow on the ground. But once it all melts ferns and lilies are popping up all over the place. We all get so excited, we head to Sunnyside Gardens to get more plants for the garden. We plant them, but then have to cover them for another frost is coming. But, the flowers are beautiful. People are ecstatic to see green grass popping up, the trees so green and beautiful and of course the flowers are lovely. The nice thing, it gives us all something to do in the spring. Planting. And, in the summer, weeding, pruning, snipping this and that and can't forget to cut the grass. And, it is all so beautiful. Let's plant a boulevard garden. Now that is cool. Anything goes. Busy, busy, buzz, buzz, save the bees for they are a necessity. There are mosquitoes too folks and little see umms. You feel them but you can't see them. They like some people more than others. And, there are rabbits and bunnies. So cute. The squirrels, chipmunks, even had a raccoon in the garage. Knocked over a can of red paint. you could see the trail he left behind. Just adds charm to the garage floor and door. Summer is so beautiful and soooo busy, that when fall comes and winter might be here or just around the corner. We can't wait to put away the rake, find the shovel or the manly snow blower. The snow is blowing, fast and furious. Time for hot chocolate with marshmallows or hot cider. Warm up. Gear up. And do it all over again. Welcome to Minnesota Nice, Ice, Extreme there is always something to do. I can't find my easel, my paints or brushes. Just some blank canvas. Nature calls.

The beginning of a project sometimes does not come easily. Nor does the ending, sometimes not wanting the end unless it has something worthy to say. Especially, to come to a complete stop. At least with a book, you can open the pages and find something new, for now there is a better understanding. An ending also gives us time to process and expand our world, our mission for the good. If that is our calling. Whatever we choose to do, make it worthwhile, fulfilling and meaningful.

I felt in 2020 the Universe was trying to tell us something. giving us a chance to redeem ourselves. When, did we deserve it? Our hearts were breaking for the atrocities that pervaded our lives. Our leaders perpetuate the madness instead of uniting and working together. Find a common ground. Some human decency, compassion, understanding and a willingness to accept our differences. Yet, we are still the same. If we haven't learned that throughout our sordid history. Then we've learned nothing. And are not deserving ourselves. We have two parties that no longer work together. Broken. Impossible. One is big money. The other is for mankind, human decency. For the good of all. But, that scares people. For they think that will come at too high a price. Or worse, we will become socialist. Is that so? Not if the new administration does what is right and for the people. All the necessities in life have been made to profit corporate. Corporate Greed. They think they are deserving because they have been able to accumulate their wealth--not honorably. But, they are not better and they are not deserving. Time to wake up and no longer accept mediocrity. And, it is time justice prevails and we learn these lessons before the end of 2020.

God gave us the gift of life. What we do with this gift. Is our gift to God. We have a forgiving God. He gave us this beautiful earth. Let's take care of our people. Let's take care of the air we breathe, the sea, the waters keep pure for the fish and fowl. The land should not be used for fracking, but farming. We could feed the world. We need to care for each other. Dismantle those guns that are meant to kill. We don't need them. In our hearts we don't want them. Not if we take care of you and me and make it we. Let›s finally learn. The Universe is trying to tell us something. God created this earth. Let's give back and be creative as best we can be. That would be good for all.

Gradation of dots...

I am thankful for all who are brave enough, bold enough and fearless too. To speak out when seeing, witnessing or experiencing acts of injustice, experienced inequity or just plain problems. Address and Correct. Sometimes it's up to us. The people. Our Voice. We the People. United, not forgotten.

I remember when I bought my condo at Lake Point. My creative spirit was awakened, for the walls were like an inviting canvas. An artist friend Susan and I collaborated ideas to transform some of the inner walls to add interest, and an old world appeal. We painted a stone archway, with a path of terracotta leading from the kitchen area into a mystical area. Another time and place. We also did an alcove area as if marbled walls, and a small powder room of golden grasses. Inviting. And Unique. Several years later, I learned questionable practices were used in the contract. I would have to sell my beautiful condo. The person who was originally interested came back two years later with an offer that would allow me to buy an affordable house. With stipulations in place. I would have to move within a month. Not enough to give this real consideration. But that is what was done back then. Was it honorable?

I would learn, the people that bought my condo, would not move in until a year later. For they took out the walls, the floors and added all new lighting. That was the thing to do back then. They wanted an open modern look. If I would have told me their plans, I never would have sold my condo. The price was too high. They could have bought any other unit for they all had amazing views. But, they chose mine. Only to demolish the inspiring murals. For whatever reason I can only surmise. From Lake Point to my little cottage house.

Only a month to move, to process and do. I would learn my little cottage house that had such appeal also came with numerous undisclosed problems. Edina Realty, the agent and all who were involved became unreachable. I even contacted the state, told them about my buying this little cottage house. The person I spoke to, told me that was a terrible experience I had. But also, was told because,"I did not work for a corporation, I was only an individual, they could not help me. I had no recourse." Only catering to large companies with big money was so morally and ethically wrong--I could not believe what I was hearing. The moral decline in transactions was now big profit for those who dare and are willing. I was not going to let this break me. I knew this was unexceptable, inexcusable and blatant too. I was determined to rise above this. Meanwhile, I decided...

To remove the wallpaper in the powder room on the main level. After I removed the wallpaper, I decided I would paint a mural of Monet Garden on these walls. My inspiration grew. My artist friend wanted to assist, for she needed some financial help. I reluctantly relented for several reasons. I felt like Michelangelo at times. We finished. That little powder room became the main attraction for many. Again this was unique.

I would live in this little cottage house for twelve years. I learned to garden. I loved the way the light poured into the rooms and onto the landing of the stairwell. My expenses continued to grow with the constant repairs and maintenance would take a toll financially, physically, emotionally too. For the constant demands for higher taxes. Regardless of the mercenaries who were constantly wanting more. All this became a labor of love. But, drained me in every way to the point I would have to sell. I paid on the principle all those years too. It didn't matter for when I sold my little cottage, I ended up selling it for less than when I bought this little house. Why did this happen?

I continued to learn lessons that I can apply to everyday life. I learned I can write, If there is a reason and purpose that will teach and inspire others also. I feel fortunate to have a creative life, for that I am thankful. Creativity comes in many forms. From painting to building, to finding solutions instead of giving up and accepting. For too long our leaders have let problems grow to profit. We all need to stay healthy, in mind, body and spirit. Be aware of what is going on around you, your family, your community, your schools.

What they teach. Is it honest and true? Are there omissions in their agenda or textbooks? Speak up when there is a feeling of doubt. Knowledge is power. And, we never stop learning. That is so exciting. So be aware of your creative gifts given to you. So take precious care.

When the pandemic struck, the Universe was telling us, teaching us, giving us a chance to get this right. We are human beings. Not a robot that is being fed information to be used for whatever purpose. Humans are better than that, for we are creative thinkers, with capabilities we go beyond when we use our gifts God has given.

*Another extension of the Monet garden theme.
There would be four walls painted with this theme.*

I missed the murals in my Lake Point Condo. When I removed the old wall paper in the powder room, I decided to paint a Monet garden theme. When finally completed became a main focal point offering artistry, charm, fascination and inspiration. Our home is an extension of ourselves. Bring out your creative self and make it beautiful.

These pastel drawings were done at home for Alan Larkins class. Random objects two books surrounded by two baseball banks at the left, to the right a shiny metal cup showing reflection, behind the cup is a pen and pencil holder and to the center is a small tea bag holder and to the right is cup and saucer with a spoon resting. All items from my South Bend home. Almost like a memorabilia keepsake.

Below this drawing, again are random drawing of items at home. Napkin folded in a ceramic ring, off to the right a ceramic cup, the center is bronze metal candle holder, to the right a glass carafe with a small sipping goblet to the right. In the center is a small decorative container, a small gold chain and bracelet and to the right and in front of the carafe is a small bottle of nail polish. Random items around the house.

Patti Zona

These drawings were done with Charcoal, the backdrop on white paper.. The top items are placed on a crumpled cloth. A study of contrast, textures and gradation of shades and shadows.

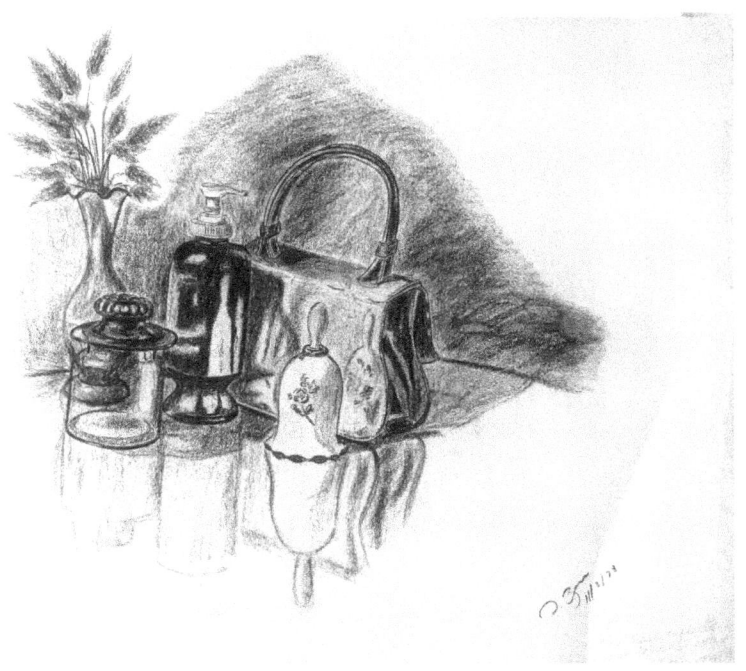

This picture is similar but on a flat surface the items placed in close proximity, the vase of wispy flora, seen through the glass jar, the shiny black atomizer reflecting the decorative bell of china and other items around it, the added silver clutch bag reflecting and deflecting adding to the interest and study. The reflection of items on the surface of the table or tableau.

I blackened the paper with charcoal and did the drawing with an eraser. Working from light to dark seems more natural than bringing out the lights from the dark. But, actually once you start, it works and there is a appreciation and understanding that is unique. The glass carafe sitting precariously close to the edge of the table, next to the brass lantern, behind the heavy bowl. The pottery gravy bowl at the end is a solid contrast, The darks to the light. I like that.

I enjoyed doing these charcoal drawings where we completely covered the papers with charcoal. So, pretty messy, but you forget about that once it begins to make sense in shape and form. Again, I had random objects of different shapes, sizes and purpose. You want to challenge yourself. Just to see what you can do or achieve. These were done on drawing papers. Can you imagine what we all could do, if we took the time, inclination to learn from our teachers. We can achieve almost anything. Just make it wonderful and worthwhile. An inspiration. With gratitude.

Also, by Patti Zona

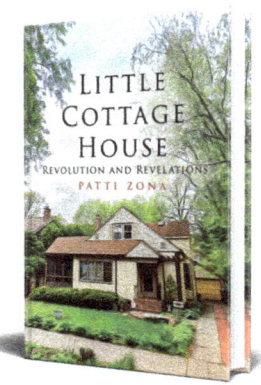  

Little Cottage House   Bohemian Momé   The Value of a Homemaker

"Patti Zona is one of the most honest and forthright voices to read today. Her insights into society's missteps are the kind of ideas that should be shouted from rooftops! Thank goodness she has the gumption to bravely point out that the emperor has no clothes."

Red Gallagher

www.ingramcontent.com/pod-product-compliance
Lightning Source LLC
Chambersburg PA
CBHW041326110526
44592CB00021B/2835